Decks 1-2-3

Design

Build

Maintain

Repair

Meredith®
BOOKS

Decks 1-2-3™ TABLE OF CONTENTS

HOW TO USE THIS BOOK

Decks 1-2-3 is filled with the step-by-step projects you need to build the deck of your dreams! Professional deck builders from The Home Depot stores across the United States provided projects that people like you want to do. They helped make sure the book has all the steps for you to successfully complete the deck and deck accessories you want.

Start by reading **Designing and Planning a Deck Project**. It will help you determine what features you want from a deck; how much and what kind of lumber, fasteners, and other materials you need for your deck; and what tools will help you do the job right.

Four Deck Projects provides an overview of the steps involved in building the four basic types of decks: single-level raised, multi-level, low-level, and ground-level. By looking at what's involved in assembling each type of deck and what each finished deck looks like, you'll have a better idea of what you want to build to fit your home and lifestyle.

Before you begin building, turn to **Laying Out a Deck**. Proper layout ensures footings and posts will be in the right place to support a strong, stable deck.

Ready to start building? **Digging and Pouring Footings** shows you how to create the proper foundation to support whatever type of deck you want.

Framing walks you through the projects involving the structural support of the deck, including the posts, beams, and joists.

Once you've dug and poured the footings, and created the structural supports for your deck, you're ready to add the **Decking**. Since decking is the most visible part of a deck, in addition to providing all the steps involved in laying deck boards, this chapter also shows you how to properly drive fasteners into deck boards for a professional-looking finish. If you want a deck surface with no visible fasteners, check out how to install decking with decking clips or a track system.

Most decks require stairs or a ramp to access the deck platform. Turn to **Building Stairs and Ramps** for how to build stairs with open and closed stringers, add a platform to break up a long series of steps, wrap stairs around a corner, and make a safe ramp.

Codes require that most decks with more than two steps have a railing. Read **Railings** for further railing code information and projects for building a safe yet stylish rail for your deck.

Decks, just like the interior of your home, can be accessorized to meet your personal style and needs. Check out **Building Deck Accessories** for projects including attaching skirting and fascia, building benches, adding a privacy screen, and making an arbor. This chapter even has tips for installing low-voltage lighting!

If you have an existing deck that needs a little sprucing up, or just want to keep your new deck in top shape, turn to **Deck Finishing, Maintenance, and Repairs**. This chapter also covers how to safely tear down an old deck if you are ready to replace an existing structure.

Decks 1-2-3 provides the step-by-step directions, tips from the pros, material and tool information, and design inspiration to help you design, build, and maintain a deck that will enhance your home and expand your outdoor living options.

TRICKS OF THE TRADE

Tips from the pros at The Home Depot® are scattered throughout this book. Their expert advice will help you successfully complete the projects in *Decks 1-2-3*.

SAFETY ALERT!
Prevent unsafe situations.

Homer's Hindsight
Avoid common mistakes.

A+ WORK SMARTER
Make smart work choices.

TRIP SAVER
Save time and mileage.

Designer Tip
Create a stylishly lit home.

TOOL TIP
Use specialty tools to their best advantage.

OOPS!
Fix common mistakes. (Not that you'll make any.)

BUYER'S GUIDE
Select the best materials.

CLOSER LOOK
Understand all the details.

DESIGNING AND PLANNING A DECK PROJECT

ELEVATION DRAWING

House

Patio Door

3¾" Space Between Balusters

4x4 Railing Posts

2x2 Balusters

2x4 Rails

36"

6x6 Posts

8'10"

7' O.C.

12" Concrete Dia. Footings

48"

Concrete Tube Form

Flared to 24"

4" Compactible Gravel

Take the time to design and plan your deck carefully. Consider how you'll use your outdoor spaces. Do you plan to barbecue on the deck? Would a hot tub be a relaxing addition? Will large groups of people gather on the deck for parties? Make certain the deck design meets as many of your desires as possible, and if you plan to add elements such as a spa in the future, make the structure strong enough now to save yourself extra work later. Read through this entire book for design ideas. A good initial plan will make your building project as easy and stress-free as possible. Plus careful planning will ensure your deck is a source of pride and satisfaction for a long time.

CHAPTER ONE PROJECTS

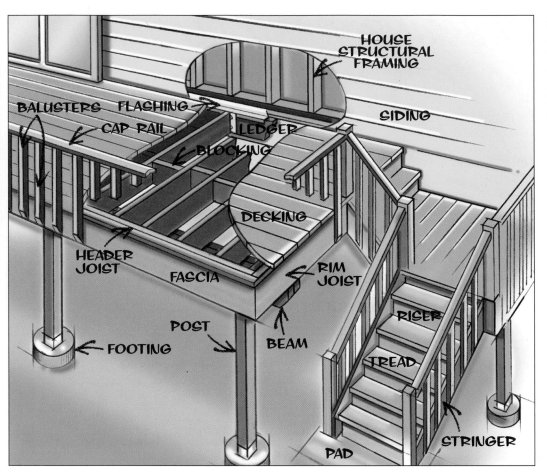

HOUSE STRUCTURAL FRAMING

BALUSTERS FLASHING

CAP RAIL

LEDGER

BLOCKING

SIDING

DECKING

HEADER JOIST

FASCIA

RIM JOIST

POST

RISER

FOOTING

BEAM

TREAD

STRINGER

PAD

A TYPICAL DECK contains these structural components. Look in the glossary below for descriptions.

TALK LIKE A PRO
Knowing these terms will help you use this book and talk with professional contractors.

Baluster: Railing member, usually vertical, that divides space between posts and rails.

Beam: Horizontal framing member, usually resting on posts, that supports joists. Frequently made from doubled pieces of 2× lumber.

Bevel: Angle other than 90° through the thickness of a piece of lumber. Also, making a cut at such an angle.

Blocking: Short lengths of lumber installed between joists to stabilize them, usually made from lumber of the same dimension as the joists.

Butt joint: Joint between square-cut ends or faces of lumber fastened together.

Cap rail: Horizontal part of railing laid flat across tops of rails or balusters.

Cure: Process where concrete fully dries and hardens.

Decking: Horizontal floor surface of a deck, or the individual pieces of lumber used for the surface (also known as deck boards).

Fascia: Decorative pieces of lumber, usually cedar or redwood, installed vertically over structural framing members.

Flashing: Metal used to protect a joint from moisture penetration, such as between ledger and house. Often purchased preformed to fit over joint.

Flush: At the same level as the surrounding or adjoining surface.

Footing: Small concrete foundation that supports a post.

Grade: The slope of the ground. Also, moving dirt to adjust ground slope.

Header joist: Structural member parallel to the ledger attached across the ends of joists.

Joist: 2× lumber set on edge that supports decking.

Kerf: Space created by the cutting path of a saw blade.

Ledger: Horizontal framing member made from 2× lumber attached to structural framing of the house.

Load: Amount of weight a deck supports. Also known as live load.

Miter: Angle other than 90° across the width of a piece of lumber. Also, making a cut at such an angle.

Pad: Concrete slab footing that supports bottom end of stairs or heavy accessory such as a spa.

Perimeter joists: Joists that form the outer edges of a deck.

Plumb: Vertical. Also, making exactly vertical.

Post: Vertical framing member, usually 4×4 or 6×6 lumber, supporting beams. Also, vertical supports for a railing.

Rim joist: 2× lumber set on edge at the outer edge of a deck.

Riser: Vertical section of a step.

Scarf joint: Joint between two lumber pieces with matching bevels cut in their ends.

Shoulder: Outer edge of a notch or cut.

Square: Surfaces that are at right angles to each other. Also, making surfaces or layout lines at right angles to each other.

Story pole: Marked piece of straight lumber used for locating multiple identical cuts or fastening positions.

Stringer: 2× lumber installed diagonally that supports steps.

Tack: Temporarily attach a piece of lumber in position.

Through post: Post that passes from a footing through the deck platform to form a support for railing, bench, or arbor.

Toenail: Drive a fastener at an angle to attach one piece of lumber to another.

Tread: Horizontal portion of a step.

DESIGNING A DECK

Think about why you want a deck. Examine each of the design issues illustrated to make certain you create a deck that meets your needs. For other design options, look through magazines and other publications. Look at decks in surrounding neighborhoods, particularly on houses similar to yours. Also check with local building inspectors for regulations that may affect your design. They are an excellent resource for soil and other ground conditions in your area that may affect construction and significantly increase costs.

HEIGHT AND LOCATION: This simple low-level deck is attached to the house at door level as a transition between house and yard. Though small, the deck offers a relaxation spot and outdoor dining and cooking space. Planters provide color and blend the structure into the landscape.

LOCATION AND SHAPE: A freestanding deck isn't attached to a house. One that's along a lakeshore or in a garden offers a quiet spot to relax away from household activities. Besides rectangular, six-sided (hexagonal) and eight-sided (octagonal) shapes are popular for freestanding decks.

STYLE AND SLOPE: A multilevel deck can make use of a slope that otherwise is not usable yard space. This deck is a series of simple platforms of varying sizes arranged down a moderate grade. The separate deck levels also serve as the steps.

STAIRS AND STORAGE: Stairs can connect levels of a multilevel deck on a slope. Each level is built as a separate deck. Only the top level of this deck is attached to the house; the remaining levels are freestanding. Benches provide seating and storage areas.

DESIGNING A DECK (CONTINUED)

HEIGHT, STYLE, AND SLOPE: A single level is a popular design for second-story decks. A steep slope requires special building techniques. A retaining wall can be built to create level ground for standard post installation (left photo). Or concrete footings can be extended above ground level as post supports with tops that are level with each other (right photo). A professional should install either of these. Also consider hiring a professional to build the framing for a deck on a steep slope. Then, you can install the decking and railing yourself.

STRUCTURE: The extension of decking over a support beam underneath is called cantilevering. The other method is to attach joists to a beam face (see bottom left photo on page 7). Cantilevering makes posts and beams less visible, but the other method uses fewer materials and provides more usable space underneath the deck.

BRACING FOR SUPPORT: Permanent post bracing for a deck may be required by local code (see page 108). Ground or weather conditions can make extra support necessary for structural rigidity.

FUNCTIONAL FORM: Creating 45-degree angles at deck corners offers a simple but visually interesting change from the traditional rectangle. Working with 45-degree angles is relatively simple. Also, metal connectors are available for installing joists at this angle (see page 18).

ACCESS AND TRAFFIC PATTERN: Minimize how far stairs protrude into a yard by installing them at a 45-degree angle to the deck. This also creates visual interest and can improve the traffic pattern, as on this deck. The angled stairs direct traffic away from the dining area.

WRAP-AROUND ACCESS: Wrapping a deck around one or more corners of a house provides convenient access from multiple spots within the house. Several separate functional spaces are created on a wraparound deck. This deck has room for a spa as well as dining and entertainment areas.

ACCESSIBILITY: Building an access ramp is similar to building a deck—it's just a deck built at an incline. Check with local code for design and building regulations applying to width and incline angles before installing an access ramp.

TRAFFIC PATTERN AND SIZE: Even a relatively large deck can be too small if its design doesn't allow for a good traffic pattern. The original deck on this house (left photo) served primarily as an oversized stairway to the pool area. Dining and

entertaining were limited because traffic flow moved directly through the main deck area. Building a new deck (right photo) that made better use of available space and routed traffic to the deck corners provided ample room for activities.

MAINSTAY WOOD: Pressure-treated lumber, the least expensive deck material, can be used for the entire deck, as was done on this deck. Notice the landing that provides a resting place on a long stair run and changes stair direction so the stairway doesn't protrude into the yard.

SURFACE MATERIALS: Cedar and redwood are decorative woods that make an attractive deck surface. Install this lumber over pressure-treated lumber, which should be used for structural framing. Cedar, coated with a clear sealant, is used on this deck.

RAILS: Any pattern or material may be used for a deck railing as long as it meets local code regulations (see page 11). Notice the variety shown on these pages and elsewhere in this book. Keep in mind that children might easily climb a railing with balusters that aren't vertical.

PRIVATE GETAWAY: A privacy screen shields deck activity from the surrounding landscape. It also provides a wind-break. Notice how the wraparound seating integrates into the privacy screen.

ACCESSORY AND STYLE: An arbor provides shade on a sun-washed deck. The amount of shade depends on the amount and pattern of the lumber used for the arbor roof. An arbor also visually divides a deck into separate activity areas and can be a foundation for climbing plants.

DISGUISED STORAGE: Cover the open area underneath a deck with a skirt. A common method is to install sections of lattice screen as shown on this deck. Include an access panel for storage areas beneath the deck.

SUPPORT ACCESSORIES: A spa, fire pit, or brick barbecue are popular additions for a deck. Support these heavy accessories with a concrete pad that positions the unit at the proper height relative to the decking.

ROOM FOR NATURE: Enclose a tree or other natural element within a deck. Decking is supported with extra framing at the opening. Check with a garden center or arboretum for the amount of growing space that must be left for a tree. An enclosed tree may require additional watering.

PLANNING A DECK PROJECT

Always check with a building inspector about local code regulations before you plan your deck. Information in this book is based on general building code regulations, but local codes always set final standards. A freestanding deck usually is subject to fewer regulations since it is not attached to the house.

On a cantilevered deck, joists can extend beyond the outer beam no more than 1/4 of their allowable span. For example, joists with a 12-foot span can extend 3 feet past the beam. Check the grade of the ground at the deck site with a level. It should slope away from the house at least 1/4 inch per foot so water drains away from the foundation. Add dirt and regrade the area if necessary.

Calculating measurements for baluster spacing or stair rise and run is easily done with a calculator. However, you may get a number after the decimal point that doesn't easily correspond to a measurement you can make with a tape measure. (See the chart below for common measurements.)

RECOMMENDED SPANS AND SPACING

MAXIMUM DISTANCE BETWEEN JOIST SUPPORTS:

Joist spacing (on center)

Joist size	12"	16"	24"
2×6	11'7"	9'9"	7'11"
2×8	15'0"	12'10"	10'6"
2×10	19'6"	16'5"	13'4"

MAXIMUM DISTANCE BETWEEN POSTS SUPPORTING BEAMS:

Joist span

Beam size	6'	8'	10'	12'
4×6	8'	7'	6'	5'
4×8	10'	9'	8'	7'
4×10	12'	11'	10'	9'
4×12	14'	13'	12'	11'

RECOMMENDED POST SIZE:

Load area*

Deck height	48	72	96	120	124
0' to 6'	4×4	4×4	6×6	6×6	6×6
6' and up	6×6	6×6	6×6	6×6	6×6

*To calculate "load area" multiply the distance between the beams by the distance between the posts (in feet).

THESE ARE TYPICAL SPAN MEASUREMENTS. Spans between framing members also depend on the species of wood used to make pressure-treated lumber. Check with a building inspector to see if span distances differ in your area.

DECIMAL EQUIVALENTS OF COMMON FRACTIONS

8THS	16THS	32NDS	EQUALS	8THS	16THS	32NDS	EQUALS
		1	.03125			17	.53125
	1	2	.0625		9	18	.5625
		3	.09375			19	.59375
1	2	4	.125	5	10	20	.625
		5	.15625			21	.65625
	3	6	.1875		11	22	.6875
		7	.21875			23	.71875
2	4	8	.25	6	12	24	.75
		9	.28125			25	.78125
	5	10	.3125		13	26	.8125
		11	.34375			27	.84375
3	6	12	.375	7	14	28	.875
		13	.40625			29	.90625
	7	14	.4375		15	30	.9375
		15	.46875			31	.96875
4	8	16	.5	8	16	32	1.0

USE THIS CHART to convert calculator decimals to fractions of an inch. Choose the conversion equivalent that is closest to the number after the decimal point shown on the calculator.

NOMINAL LUMBER SIZES

NOMINAL SIZE	ACTUAL SIZE
2×2	1½×1½
2×4	1½×3½
2×6	1½×5½
2×8	1½×7¼
2×10	1½×9¼
2×12	1½×11¼
4×4	3½×3½
6×6	5½×5½

LUMBER IS IDENTIFIED by its nominal size, which is its rough dimension before it is trimmed to finished size at the lumber mill. Actual sizes are approximate lumber dimensions after trimming. Use actual size dimensions when calculating spacing.

2x6 BEAM & JOIST

DECKING PATTERNS

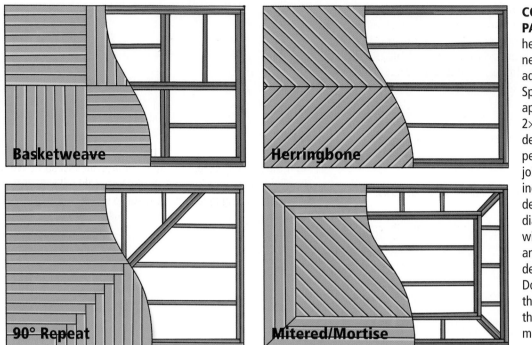

Basketweave

Herringbone

90° Repeat

Mitered/Mortise

COMMON DECKING PATTERNS are shown here with the framing necessary for adequate support. Space joists 16 inches apart on center for 2×4, 2×6, or ⁵⁄₄×6 decking installed perpendicular to the joists. Space joists 12 inches apart for ⁵⁄₄×6 decking installed diagonally. Mixing 2×4 with 2×6 decking is another appealing design possibility. Don't use boards wider than 6 inches since they cup and split more easily.

CALCULATING STAIRS

RISE

RUN

RISE is the vertical distance between stair treads. Run is the horizontal distance of each tread. Make these measurements consistent on a stair run. The best combination of rise and run measurements is between 17 and 21 inches. Ideal rise distance is 6 to 7 inches but never more than 8 inches. Overall rise is stair height. Overall run is the length of the stair run.

Calculate a stair run based on the planned height of the deck. After the deck and pad are built, recalculate using actual distances before cutting stringers. An 11-inch tread distance is typical. The number of treads is one less than the number of risers—the top "tread" is the deck surface.

1. Divide overall rise by desired rise per step—use either 6 or 7 inches. This gives you an estimated number of steps. (Ex.: 46 ÷ 6 = 7.67 steps)

2. Round up or down to the closest whole number. (Ex.: 8 steps)

3. Divide overall rise by number of steps to get actual rise per step. (Ex.: 46 ÷ 8 = 5.75 or 5³⁄₄ inches rise per step)

4. If this rise distance isn't acceptable, either add or subtract one step and recalculate. (Ex.: 46 ÷ 7 = 6.57 or about 6⁹⁄₁₆ inches rise per step—see the Decimal Conversion Chart, page 9)

5. If the final rise distance is approximate, one rise measurement will be slightly different. Place this rise at the bottom of the stair run. (Ex.: Using 6⁹⁄₁₆ for rise measurements makes the bottom rise about 6⁵⁄₈ inches)

CALCULATING RAILINGS

Position posts between 4 and 6 feet apart. Make the distance between posts as consistent as possible. Codes require that no space between railing members may be more than 4 inches. This includes the space between the decking and a bottom rail if one is installed. To be safe, use a 3³/₄ inch spacing to calculate railings.

1. Add the width of a baluster (i.e.: 1.5 inches) to the desired spacing.
(Ex.: 1.5 + 3.75 = 5.25)

2. Divide this into the total distance between posts.
(Ex.: 70 ÷ 5.25 = 13.34)

3. Round to the nearest whole number to find the number of balusters. (Ex.: 13)

4. Multiply this by the width of one baluster. (Ex.: 13 × 1.5 = 19.5)

5. Subtract this from the total distance between posts. (Ex.: 70 – 19.5 = 50.5)

6. Add 1 to the number of balusters to find the number of spacings. (Ex.: 13 + 1 = 14)

7. Divide this into the remainder from step 5 to find the actual spacing measurement between balusters. (Ex.: 50.5 ÷ 14 = 3.6 or 3⁵/₈ inches, see Decimal Conversion Chart, p. 9)

8. If the spacing distance is approximate, the last space will be slightly different. This will not be noticeable. (Ex.: Using 3⁵/₈ inch spacing means the last space will be about 3¹/₂ inches)

DRAWING BUILDING PLANS

A building inspector usually will need to see a plot drawing (top illustration, also known as a floor-plan drawing) and an elevation (bottom illustration) before approving your deck project. The plot drawing is an overhead view of the deck with ledger, footing, beam, joist, and stair sizes and locations. Spacing and distance measurements and decking pattern also should be shown. Make more than one drawing to include all of this information if necessary. The elevation drawing is a side view of the deck showing footing depth, deck height, and railing spacings. These plans should accurately reflect your deck plan, but they don't have to be professional quality. Use graph paper and convert actual distances with a ¹/₄ inch = 1 foot scale that fits on the paper. Or use the computer plan-drawing system at your local building center if available.

Minimize waste by designing your deck to take advantage of stock lumber sizes as much as possible. The plans will help you estimate how much material will be needed for building the deck. Plans will also help you figure the lengths of decking to buy if the deck is wider than what can be spanned with one board.

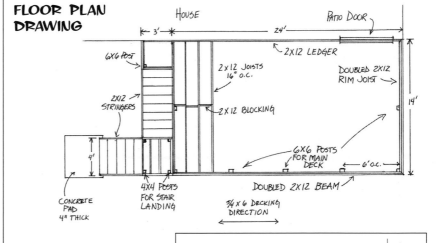

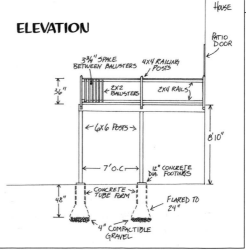

ESTIMATING MATERIALS

ESTIMATING LUMBER

Count the number of each size piece necessary from your building plan for the framing members, stairs, and railings. Calculate the decking necessary based on the actual width of the boards you will use. Don't forget to allow for the gap between boards. Stock decking lengths won't line up with joist spacing on a wide deck. Figure the lengths necessary to fit the joist spacing with minimum amount of waste. Add 10 percent to each category for normal building waste. (Add 15 percent to the decking category if installing it diagonally.)

ESTIMATING CONCRETE

For Round Footings:

1. Multiply half the diameter of the hole in inches times itself. (Ex.: For a 12 inch hole this would be $6 \times 6 = 36$)

2. Multiply this by 3.14. (Ex.: $36 \times 3.14 = 113.04$)

3. Multiply this by the depth of the hole in inches. (Ex.: $113.04 \times 48 = 5425.9$)

4. Divide this by 1728 to find the cubic feet of concrete required. (Ex.: $5425.9 \div 1728 = 3.14$ cubic feet of concrete for one 12-inch-diameter hole that is 48 inches deep)

5. A 60-pound bag of premixed concrete contains .5 cubic feet so divide the total cubic feet needed for all footings by .5 to find the number of bags needed—or relay the total feet needed to a concrete supplier for delivery of ready-mixed concrete (see page 69).

For Rectangular Pads and Footings:

1. Multiply the length times the width of the area in inches. (Ex.: $36 \times 36 = 1296$)

2. Multiply this by the depth of the area in inches. (Ex.: $1296 \times 4 = 5184$)

3. Divide this by 1728 to find the cubic feet of concrete required. (Ex.: $5184 \div 1728 = 3$ cubic feet of concrete for a 36×36 pad that is 4 inches thick)

4. See step 5 under "Estimating Concrete."

ESTIMATING HARDWARE

Count the number of metal connectors and fasteners necessary for the framing (see page 16). Estimate 5 pounds of screws (or nails) for every 100 square feet of decking.

SCHEDULING THE PROJECT

Know your building site. Heavy clay, rocky, or sandy soils will affect project timing. Anticipate rain that may collapse footing holes. Tree roots, rock shelves, or a high water table are problems that may require professional attention.

Have lumber delivered a couple of weeks before you build. Cover it with plastic so it stays dry while it adjusts to local moisture conditions. A pad can require a large amount of concrete. Schedule a pad installation so the concrete for it is delivered at the same time as the concrete for footings if possible.

THE BUILDING INSPECTOR usually will inspect your project at several steps in the building process. Find out when these inspections must take place and allow for them in your building schedule. Here the inspector is checking for proper footing depth.

CHOOSING MATERIALS

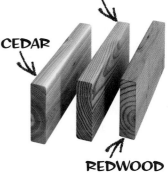

PRESSURE-TREATED

CEDAR

REDWOOD

Use pressure-treated lumber for framing. It provides greater structural strength and costs less than other building materials. Use it to frame even if you don't like its looks, then choose a material you like for the decking, railings, and other visible surfaces.

Cedar and redwood are commonly used for exposed deck surfaces. They are more expensive than pressure-treated, which can be used for the entire deck. If you like the looks of cedar or redwood, don't assume it's out of your budget. Depending on the size of your deck, the cost for a lumber upgrade may be less than you'd expect. Composite materials also are available for decking and railings. Though they are more expensive than wood, they generally require less maintenance than lumber. Arrange to purchase all composite materials from the same dye lot to get consistent color. Plan ahead—they usually require special ordering. Decking is usually 2×6 or ⁵⁄₄×6 boards. Radius-edged ⁵⁄₄×6 boards mean the edges on each board are rounded.

2×6

⁵⁄₄×6

Before choosing wood for visible surfaces, test how finish products look on scrap wood pieces. Cedar or redwood may not be worth the extra expense if you will cover them with opaque stain or paint. You may choose to leave deck wood unfinished and let it weather. Weathering usually takes a few months with cedar or redwood, a year or two with pressure-treated lumber.

Plan for approximately 10 percent waste when purchasing lumber for a deck. Check the home center's return policy in case you don't use it all. Also check delivery and pickup fees. Few do-it-yourselfers have a vehicle adequate to transport all the building materials for a deck. (See pages 16–18 for other materials and fasteners necessary for deck building.)

SAFETY ALERT!

Always wear eye protection, a dust mask, and long clothes when cutting pressure-treated lumber. Avoid tracking shavings into the house.

COMPOSITE DECK MATERIALS, made from a combination of wood products and recycled plastic, are used for decking and railing. Cut and fasten composite materials with the same tools and methods used with wood.

Designer Tip

Opaque stains, tinted to wood tones or other colors, provide heavy coverage and are the best choice for pressure-treated lumber (right, top row). A semitransparent stain tinted to a light wood tone creates an even color on cedar or redwood without hiding the wood (right, bottom row). A clear finish emphasizes the wood's natural beauty. Cedar weathers to silver-gray and redwood weathers to brown-gray.

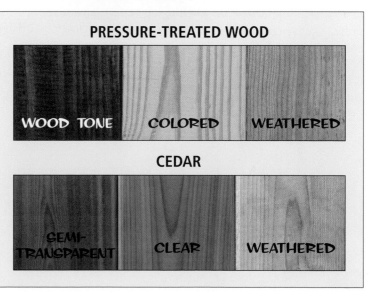

PRESSURE-TREATED WOOD

WOOD TONE | COLORED | WEATHERED

CEDAR

SEMI-TRANSPARENT | CLEAR | WEATHERED

SELECTING LUMBER

WORKING WITH WET LUMBER

The lumber you purchase may be wet, depending on where it was stored. You can work with wet lumber or, if you have the time, allow the boards to dry for a couple of weeks. Wet lumber will shrink as it dries, so butt decking boards tightly together, or you'll have huge gaps when the wood is dry. Never mix wet and dry boards because you'll have uneven spacing once all the boards dry.

LOOK DOWN THE LENGTH OF A BOARD to check for warps and twists. Also check for the "crown" edge. Some boards may have a slight bow along one edge. The middle of the board will be crowned, or higher than the ends. Mark this edge and install it upward. The board will straighten over time.

MEASURE THE WIDTH of each board before cutting and installing. Don't assume boards are the named size. There may be as much as 3/8-inch difference between two boards of the same labeled dimension—especially true of pressure-treated lumber.

REJECT BOARDS with insect holes, rot, mildew, or pockets of sap.

LOOK FOR MARKS left by milling machines when the lumber was made. Reject the board unless you can cut off the damaged part and still have a usable length.

REJECT BOARDS with severe warps or twists. Warped boards have an evenly curved surface. Diagonal corners curl the same direction on twisted boards.

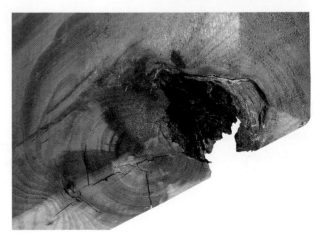

EXAMINE EVERY KNOT. Tight knots usually are acceptable. Don't use boards with knots at the edges for framing. Cut off portions with loose or missing knots. Also remove knots that are surrounded by dark rings—they may fall out later.

WORK SMARTER

GIVE IT A QUICK DIP
Coat freshly cut surfaces on pressure-treated lumber with preservative. The pressure treatment isn't always absorbed completely through the wood, especially in 4× and larger lumber. Dipping cut ends in a bucket containing preservative is simple (near right). Brush preservative on surfaces cut in place (far right).

LOOK FOR CHECKS AND SPLITS. A check is a crack going partway through the lumber; a split goes completely through. Cut off the damaged portion.

A SHAKE is a separation between growth rings along the face of a board. Remove the damaged section.

CUT OFF A PORTION with untrimmed bark (called a wane).

REMOVE A SECTION with missing wood along the edge or corner, also called a wane. If the board has a good face and two good edges, it's okay to place the wane face-down.

CHOOSING OTHER MATERIALS

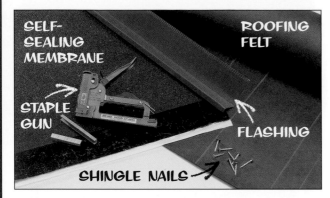

SELF-SEALING MEMBRANE

ROOFING FELT

STAPLE GUN

FLASHING

SHINGLE NAILS

INSTALL MOISTURE AND VAPOR BARRIERS to protect deck and house framing. Place building paper behind a ledger when you remove existing siding material (see page 45). Attach strips of self-sealing membrane over the top seam between boards of built-up beams. Attach these materials with staples or shingle nails. Install flashing over the top edge of a ledger (see pages 45–46).

MAKE FOOTINGS AND STAIR PADS from concrete. If you mix concrete, 60- and 90-pound bags are available, but consider having ready-mixed concrete delivered (see page 69). Regular concrete mix is suitable for most situations. Fast-setting concrete mix contains an accelerator that speeds the curing process. Sand mix doesn't contain gravel and can be smoothed to a thin edge for a transition for an access ramp. It is not strong enough for other uses.

SELECTING FASTENERS

Always use corrosion-resistant fasteners to build a deck. Galvanized fasteners are the most common and the least expensive. Stainless-steel fasteners are expensive, but they are rustproof. Use only stainless-steel fasteners in redwood. Materials in other fasteners react with natural chemicals in redwood and cause unattractive dark streaks. Nails or screws are fastening options for decking. Fasten framing with screws and bolts (or manufacturer-specified nails used with metal connectors, see page 17).

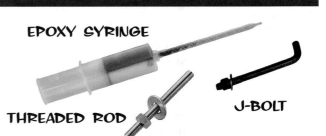

EPOXY SYRINGE

THREADED ROD

J-BOLT

74). Threaded rod comes in precut lengths in $\frac{1}{2}$- and $\frac{5}{8}$-inch diameters with a nut and washer. To avoid mangling the threads when installing the rod, put a nut on the end of the rod, then tap the rod into the hole with a hammer. Epoxy bonds the rod in the hole. Epoxy is available in a syringe that mixes ingredients. A J-bolt also may be used but it must be inserted in the footing when the concrete is wet (see page 74).

LAG SCREWS
are large-diameter screws used to fasten framing. A screw should

CARRIAGE BOLT

LAG SCREW

penetrate into framing a distance equal to twice the thickness of the piece being fastened. Large-diameter bolts also are used when there is access to both ends of the fastener. Carriage bolts have a rounded head. Machine bolts have a hexagonal-sided head similar to that on lag screws. Choose a bolt length at least 1 inch longer than the combined thickness of the pieces to be bolted together.

INSTALLING A THREADED ROD into a hole drilled at least 4 inches deep in a concrete footing is the easiest method to accurately attach a metal post anchor (see page

DECK SCREWS ARE THE BEST CHOICE
for deck applications. Use deck screws long enough to penetrate framing to a depth at least equal to the thickness of the piece they fasten. Drive deck screws with a drill and a screw tip that

SPIRAL SHANK NAILS

DECK SCREWS

SCREW TIPS

matches the slotted head of the screws. Use 3$\frac{1}{4}$- or 3$\frac{1}{2}$-inch spiral shank nails for any nailing necessary. They resist wood movement and are difficult to remove.

WORK SMARTER

NO SPLIT NAILING
Blunt the point of a nail before driving it at the end of a board or when toenailing. Rest the nailhead on a hard surface and strike the point with a hammer (near right). This slightly flattens the nail point (far right). A blunt point won't split the wood as easily as a sharp point will.

BLUNT POINT

CHOOSING METAL CONNECTORS

Metal connectors make the strongest connection between framing members. Many local codes require their use, and special connectors are necessary in earthquake and hurricane zones. Attach connectors with fasteners specified by the manufacturer. These fasteners often are short and thick galvanized nails. Fill each hole in the connector with a fastener. Never use roofing nails in fasteners. Deck clips are metal connectors used for fastening decking to joists "invisibly" (see page 133).

ADJUSTABLE POST ANCHOR attaches post to footing, allows about ½-inch adjustment in any direction of post location on footing, raises the post end away from ground moisture.

NONADJUSTABLE POST CAP is a one-piece connector that attaches beam to top of post, usually on 4×4 posts.

ADJUSTABLE POST CAP is a two-piece connector that attaches the beam to top of post, usually on posts larger than 4×4.

RAFTER TIE attaches 2× lumber joist or rafter to the top of the beam between beam ends.

SEISMIC TIE attaches 2× lumber joist or rafter to the top of the beam at beam ends.

CHOOSING METAL CONNECTORS (CONTINUED)

JOIST HANGER attaches 2× lumber joist to face of ledger or beam, available for single and double joists.

45-DEGREE JOIST HANGER attaches 2× lumber joist at 45-degree angle to face of ledger or beam; available in left- and right-hand facing pieces.

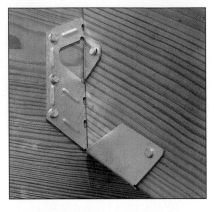

SKEWABLE JOIST HANGER, also known as rafter or stringer hanger. Attaches 2× lumber to face of framing at an adjustable angle.

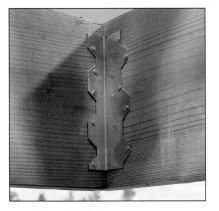

ANGLE BRACKET reinforces joint when framing members meet at a corner. Use as large a bracket as will fit or stack two smaller brackets.

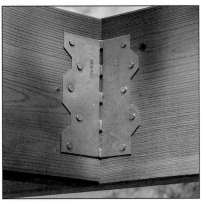

SKEWABLE ANGLE BRACKET reinforces joint at angle other than 45-degree or an angled joint at a corner where 45-degree joist hanger won't work.

JOIST TIE reinforces connection of 2× lumber to post as part of a sandwiched beam.

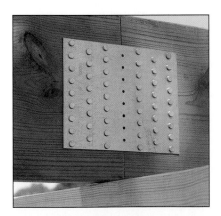

STRAPPING PLATE, also known as nailing plate, reinforces spliced joint between 2× lumber pieces.

T-STRAP reinforces connection between beam and post, and may be used in place of post cap.

STAIR BRACKET attaches tread pieces to face of closed stringer (shown) or invisibly to open stringer (see page 142).

BASIC TOOL KIT: HAND TOOLS

Building a deck is a great home improvement project because it doesn't require expensive specialty tools. If it's your first major home improvement project, it will be an opportunity to build a basic tool kit for other projects. Most of the tools are already in your tool chest if you've built home improvement projects before. The few you might not have, such as **mason's string**, a **line level**, a heavy **plumb bob,** and a **water level** (see page 24) are inexpensive. These tools are used in laying out footing positions and deck heights.

Buy the best tools you can afford. They will help you do better quality work, and they last longer. Take care of tools by cleaning and drying them after use. Keep cutting edges sharp. Dull, dirty, or rusty tools deteriorate quickly, are more difficult to use, and produce poor results. Also the risk of injury is greater because you must use greater force while using them.

You'll also need a **20- to 30-foot tape measure.** For best accuracy use the same tape measure to transfer a measured length onto a board; there may be discrepancies between different tape measures. You'll need a **50- to 100-foot tape measure** to lay out a large deck.

Speed squares, a **framing square**, a **bevel gauge,** and a long **straightedge** are used for layout and marking. A speed square makes quick work of accurately marking lumber for straight or angled cuts. It also is an excellent cutting guide when using a circular saw. The large speed square is necessary for 2×10 and larger lumber. Mark long lines by snapping a **chalk line**. A **carpenter's level** establishes level and plumb framing. Both 2-foot and 4-foot lengths are useful when building a deck. A **speed level** is handy for plumbing posts.

A **16-ounce** (minimum) **framing hammer** drives

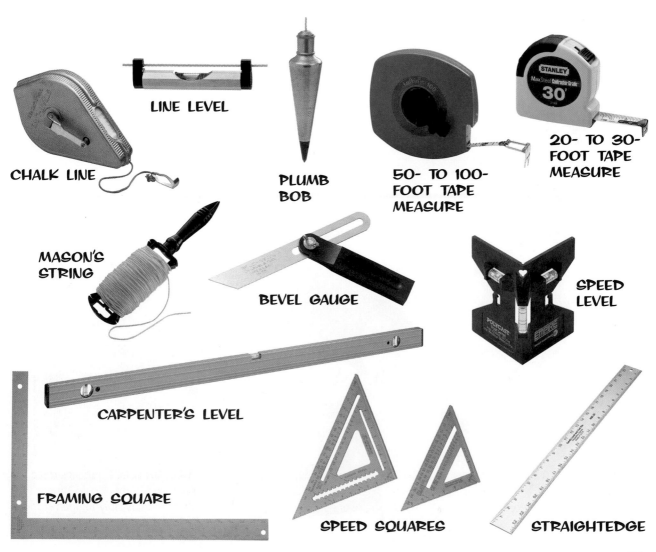

LINE LEVEL

CHALK LINE

PLUMB BOB

50- TO 100-FOOT TAPE MEASURE

20- TO 30-FOOT TAPE MEASURE

MASON'S STRING

BEVEL GAUGE

SPEED LEVEL

CARPENTER'S LEVEL

FRAMING SQUARE

SPEED SQUARES

STRAIGHTEDGE

nails and has other general uses on a building site. Drive the heads of nails flush with decking surfaces using a **nail set**. Pound stakes with a **3-pound maul**.

Install lag screws and bolts easily with a **socket and ratchet**. You may find the socket extension necessary. Use a **wrench** when you can't use the socket and ratchet.

Use a **pry bar** as a lever to shift lumber positions. A **cat's paw** is a type of pry bar used for removing embedded nails.

A **utility knife** has many uses on any building project. A **chisel** and **handsaw** often are necessary for cutting notches or completing power saw cuts.

Cut flashing with **tin snips**. Apply caulk with a **caulk gun**. A throwaway **foam brush** is useful for applying preservative to freshly cut surfaces on pressure-treated lumber. Sweep sawdust from deck surfaces with a **stiff-bristle push broom**. It also is used to texture the surface of a ground-level concrete pad. A pair of **sawhorses** are useful for supporting lumber. Several **clamps** will be helpful for holding lumber in position. Break up hard soil with a long **pinch bar** (like a heavy, straight crowbar).

Safety gear you should have on hand: **safety glasses or goggles**, **earplugs or earmuff protectors**, a **dust mask**, and **work gloves** and **boots**.

FRAMING HAMMER

NAIL SET

WRENCH

SOCKET AND RATCHET

3-POUND MAUL

UTILITY KNIFE

CAULK GUN

CHISEL

QUICK CLAMP

FOAM BRUSH

HANDSAW

PRY BAR

TIN SNIPS

CAT'S PAW

SAWHORSE

STIFF-BRISTLE PUSH BROOM

BASIC TOOL KIT: POWER TOOLS

You may already have the basic power tools necessary for deck building. If you don't, buy quality tools that are powerful, accurate, and durable. As you compare power tools, remember that the lower the amperage, the less power a tool will have. As with hand tools, keep power tools and the accessories clean, dry, and rust-free. Sharp saw blades and drill bits work better and are safer to use than dull blades and bits. Specialty power tools are shown in appropriate sections of this book. Rent them for the short time they are needed.

Power tools you'll need: The workhorse for deck building is a **circular saw**. A saw using either $6\frac{1}{2}$-inch or $7\frac{1}{4}$-inch blades works well. See pages 28 and 30 for saw blades used in deck building. Use a **power miter saw** when many straight cuts are needed, especially miters and bevels. Make cuts for stair railings that attach to deck railings at angles other than 90 degrees with a **compound miter saw**

(see page 26). A **jigsaw** makes smooth cuts in tight areas. Use a **reciprocating saw** for making cuts in framing that can't be cut with a circular saw.

Having both a **cordless drill** and a **corded drill** is useful. A cordless drill provides freedom of movement. Choose one with two batteries and a one-hour charger. The unending power of a corded drill is best for repetitive work such as driving deck screws when fastening decking. A special corded drill, called a **screwgun**, automatically sets deck screws to the proper depth. Make holes in concrete with a **hammer drill**. Drills use an assortment of **drill bits** and **screw tips**. A hammer drill uses larger heavy-duty masonry bits that are ideal for making holes in concrete.

Use a **GFCI-protected extension cord** when operating corded power tools outdoors. A **laser level**, which can be rented, can make deck layout easier.

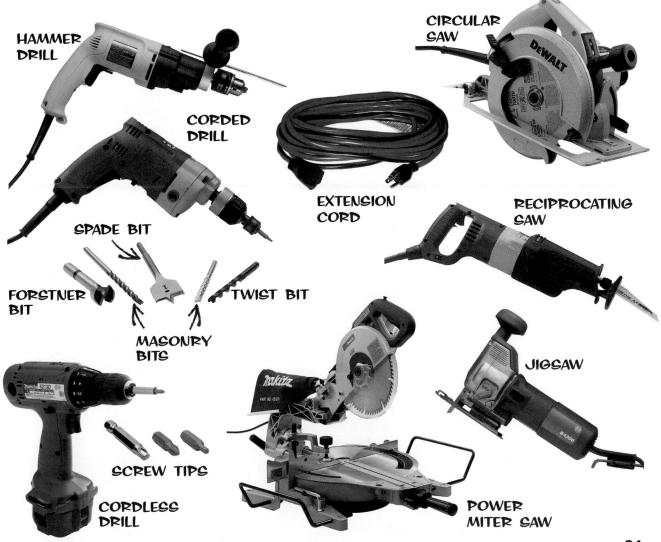

HAMMER DRILL

CORDED DRILL

CIRCULAR SAW

EXTENSION CORD

RECIPROCATING SAW

SPADE BIT

FORSTNER BIT

TWIST BIT

MASONRY BITS

JIGSAW

SCREW TIPS

CORDLESS DRILL

POWER MITER SAW

WORK LIKE A PRO

Set up a work area for greatest efficiency and accuracy. Make a miter saw platform from saw horses and 2× lumber (below, left). Place cutting supports about 3 feet on both sides of the saw. Make the top of the supports level with the saw table surface. Use a portable roller support stand when cutting long pieces of lumber (below, right). The height of the stand is adjustable and the roller top makes positioning the lumber easy.

CUTTING SUPPORTS

ROLLER SUPPORT STAND

SAFETY ALERT!

SAFETY GEAR

Use appropriate safety gear and follow proper safety procedures when building a deck:

• Wear hearing and eye protection when using all power tools

• Wear eye protection when using striking tools

• Wear a dust mask when cutting lumber and mixing concrete

• Wear gloves and work boots when handling lumber and concrete. (DO NOT wear gloves when operating power saws)

• Use GFCI-protected power cords when operating power tools outdoors.

Secure a ladder carefully before using it. Make certain both feet are firmly planted. Drive stakes on the down-grade side of the feet if there is any slope to the ground (above, left). Strap or rope the top end of a ladder to framing or another unmovable object when more than 8 feet from the ground (above, right). Or use a ladder support, a wide piece that attaches to the top of the ladder, to brace the ladder against the house. Make sure that your weight, plus whatever you carry up the ladder, doesn't exceed the maximum safe load for the ladder. Scaffolding is a more stable and safer option for working high off the ground (see page 101). It's relatively inexpensive to rent and also makes work easier and quicker.

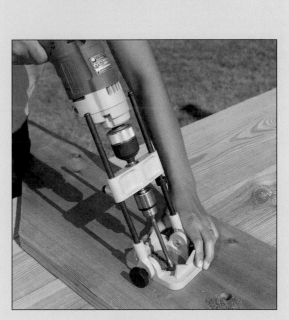

A+ WORK SMARTER

SHARP DIGGING

Sharpen the digging edges on a posthole digger or shovel with a metal file. Remove dings and rolled-over edges. Sharp digging tools slice through small roots and cut into the soil much more easily than dull tools.

TOOL TIP

DRILL GUIDE

Use a portable drill guide when you need to drill a hole at a precise angle. The guide is adjustable from 90 degrees (vertical) to 45 degrees. It attaches to either a cordless or corded drill.

QUICK-CHANGE ARTIST

In the past, pros found it most efficient to use two cordless drills when driving screws. One drill had a bit the correct size to make pilot holes. The other drill had the proper screw tip to drive the screws. Now a combination drill-and-drive attachment makes one drill perform like two. The attachment fits into a drill chuck and a slip sleeve locks in a reversible tip. One end of the tip contains a drill bit and counter sink (near right). After drilling the pilot hole, push the sleeve toward the tip to

release it. The reverse end of the tip contains the screw tip to drive a screw that fits the pilot hole (below, right). Replace the tip and push the sleeve back to lock it in.

SLIP SLEEVE →

USING A WATER LEVEL

A water level is a more accurate tool than mason's string and a line level for laying out and building a large deck. It also is especially helpful when building a deck of any size around a house corner.

One option is to buy a water level with a battery-powered electronic sensor. It emits a signal when level is reached, which is handy if you work alone. Follow manufacturer's directions for connecting the sensor.

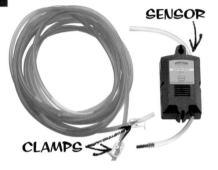

SENSOR

CLAMPS

1 **SIPHON WATER** from a bucket into the tubing. To get water into the tubing without air bubbles, clamp the lower end of the tubing when water begins to flow from it. Tinting the water with food coloring may make it easier to see.

2 **CLAMP THE TOP END** of the tubing when water is several inches from the end.

LEVELING POINT

3 **POSITION ONE END** over the point to which you are leveling. Open the clamp. Raise or lower the tubing until the water level is aligned with the leveling point. Tape tubing in place. Drive a screw or nail temporarily through the clamp to hold the weight of the water-filled tubing.

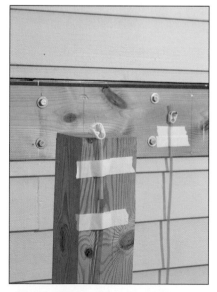

4 **LOWER THE FREE END** of the tubing until it is slightly below the leveling point. Move to the spot you are leveling. Open the clamp and slowly raise the free end. Monitor the other end of the tubing. Stop raising the free end when the water level line at the other end is aligned with the leveling point. Tape the tubing in place.

5 **MAKE A MARK** at the water level line in the tubing. Double-check that the water level line at the other end of the tubing is still aligned with the leveling point. Slowly raise or lower the free end slowly to adjust water level lines, if necessary.

POWER MITER SAW OPTIONS

SAFE MITER SAW
A 10-inch miter saw usually won't cut completely through a 2×6 at 90 degrees. Use a hand saw to finish these cuts to be safe.

A 12-INCH POWER MITER SAW will cut completely through a 2×6 at a 45° angle. This size saw is handy for making many mitered decking and railing cuts.

THE CUTTING HEAD on a sliding compound miter saw moves along a short rail. This enables it to cut completely through a 2×10 with only an 8-inch blade. This type of saw is usually more expensive.

BUYER'S GUIDE

GET THE RIGHT (OR LEFT) SAW
Circular saws are available with the saw blade mounted on either the right or left side of the motor (near right). A right-handed person using a saw with a blade on the right side must look over the saw body to see the cutting path (far right). This is awkward and may cause inaccurate cuts. If you buy a new saw, purchase one that fits the way you work. Cordless circular saws are good for making cuts in tight spaces, though they don't work for cutting many boards. Purchase the best saw you can afford. Pick the tool up and test it for fit—some saws may be too heavy for you to safely and comfortably use.

USING A COMPOUND MITER SAW

Using a compound miter saw is the easiest way to make one cut that is a combination of bevel and miter angles. This type of cut is common when installing a railing or other structure at an angle other than 90 degrees to the deck. A compound miter saw is more expensive than a power miter saw but it can be rented.

1 **MARK A CUTTING LINE** on a scrap board of the same dimension as the one that will be installed. Shown at right is an angled stair railing installation. Temporarily position the scrap board. Determine both angles at which it must be cut. The angle of the board relative to vertical will be the miter angle of the saw blade. The angle of the board relative to horizontal will be the bevel angle of the blade. Use a bevel gauge if necessary (see page 27).

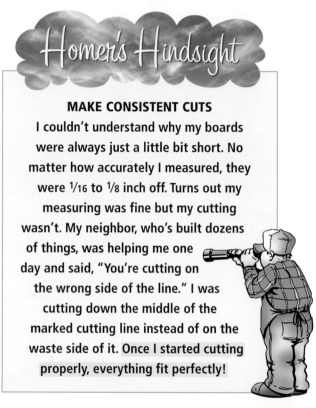

Homer's Hindsight

MAKE CONSISTENT CUTS
I couldn't understand why my boards were always just a little bit short. No matter how accurately I measured, they were 1/16 to 1/8 inch off. Turns out my measuring was fine but my cutting wasn't. My neighbor, who's built dozens of things, was helping me one day and said, "You're cutting on the wrong side of the line." I was cutting down the middle of the marked cutting line instead of on the waste side of it. Once I started cutting properly, everything fit perfectly!

2 **MAKE THE CUT** after setting the miter and bevel angles of the saw blade. Cut about 1/4 inch on the waste side of the line to see if the cut lines up correctly. Test fit the scrap piece. Make adjustments as necessary until the scrap piece fits properly. Be consistent when cutting. Either leave the line or take the line every time. Decide which method to use before you start marking boards, then mark consistently.

3 **CUT THE ACTUAL BOARD** with the blade at its final settings from Step 2. First temporarily position the board to mark the cutting length. Then attach the board after cutting it. Use deck screws to hold the joint tight.

TOOL TIP

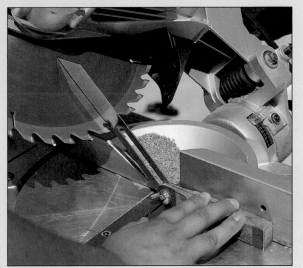

GET THE RIGHT ANGLE WITH THE RIGHT TOOL

Determine an unknown cutting angle with a bevel gauge. Loosen the wing nut on the gauge. Place the gauge handle on one surface and align the blade with the other surface forming the angle (above, left). Tighten the wing nut to hold the blade in this position. Use the gauge to mark the angle on a board, or use it to set the cutting angle of a miter saw blade. Place the gauge handle on the saw table and adjust the saw blade to match the angle made by the gauge (above, right). This also can be done with a circular saw. **Caution: Unplug the saw before checking angles.**

A SMARTER SPEED SQUARE

Make straight cuts across boards using a speed square to guide the cut. Know where to position the speed square without aligning it each time by trial and error. Use the square to guide a test cut across the end of a scrap board (near right). Mark a line on the board down the edge of the speed square. Measure between the blade kerf and the line (far right). Note the measurement and use it to position the square relative to the waste side of the cutting line whenever you guide a cut with the square. Make another test cut and measurement when you replace a blade.

CHECKING SAW BLADE ANGLES

POSITION THE WIDE EDGE of a speed square on the circular saw base (or on a miter saw table). Fully extend the blade at its vertical setting—usually the '0' mark on the miter scale. Slide the right-angle edge of the square against the side of the blade between carbide teeth. The side of the blade should be in contact with the edge of the square along its entire length. If it isn't, adjust the blade angle until it is and make a new '0' mark on the scale.

CHECK THE ANGLE of a 45-degree cut with a speed square. Adjust the saw blade angle if the cut isn't an accurate 45 degrees. Make a new 45-degree mark on the saw scale.

A+ WORK SMARTER

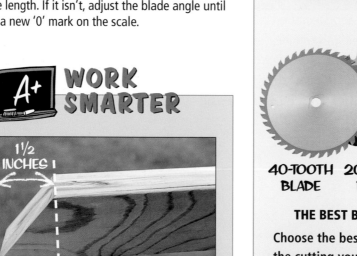

KNOW WHERE TO BEVEL

Cutting a 45-degree bevel through 2× lumber leaves a cut 1½ inches long. Circular saw blades angle in one direction. You may be forced to make a 45-degree bevel cut from the side of the board opposite that on which the cutting line is marked. Use this measurement to accurately locate the blade position when cutting from the opposite side. Make a bevel cut in one end of a board and then cut the board to length whenever possible.

BUYER'S $ GUIDE

| 40-TOOTH BLADE | 20-TOOTH BLADE | MASONRY BLADE | FINISH BLADE |

THE BEST BLADES MAKE THE BEST CUTS

Choose the best 7¼-inch circular saw blade for the cutting you do: A 40-tooth carbide-tip blade makes clean-edge miter cuts, bevel cuts, and crosscuts (cutting across the board grain). A 20-tooth carbide-tip blade is for general cutting. A masonry blade cuts concrete and stucco. A finish blade makes very smooth cuts in fascia and for other visible joints. Use a metal cutting blade, made from material similar to that used in a masonry blad but marked as a blade for metal, to cut metal siding. The tooth count is higher for miter saws. For example, a 10-inch blade for general cutting has 30 to 40 teeth. Don't use a masonry blade in a miter saw.

TOOL TIP

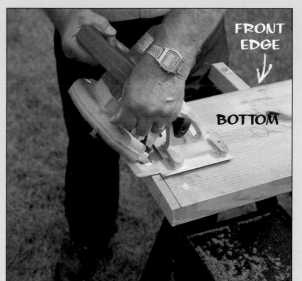

CIRCULAR SAW SUPPORT

Support the base underneath the motor of a circular saw to make the most accurate cuts, especially when making bevel cuts. It is difficult to control a saw when the base isn't fully supported (above, left). If you need to make a cut that requires leaving the saw base unsupported, flip the board (above, right). Move to the other side of the board. Make the cut from the original edge so it is at the correct angle. Adjust the position of the cutting line to cut the board to the proper length (see page 28).

THE STRAIGHT STORY

Long straight cuts are difficult to make accurately with a circular saw. Make a cutting guide with a long straightedge and a couple of clamps (near right). However, the clamps may be enough higher than the straightedge to interfere with the saw. Cut going in the opposite direction or move the clamps slightly. Or buy a straightedge guide (far right) that is self-clamping and available in various lengths.

USING A RECIPROCATING SAW

REST THE BASE of the saw shoe against the piece to be cut. This controls the cut and prevents vibration. Mount a blade with the teeth facing down for general cutting. The blade moves back and forth along its length. Use a blade long enough to pass completely through the lumber while cutting.

MAKE CUTS against obstacles by mounting the blade in the saw so the teeth face up. Rest the base of the saw shoe against the piece to be cut. Cut carefully so the blade doesn't damage other materials.

BUYER'S GUIDE

THE RIGHT RECIPROCATING SAW BLADE FOR THE JOB

Choose the proper reciprocating saw blade for the cut you make. Blades with fewer teeth cut faster but make rougher cuts. More teeth means a slower, smoother cut. Some blades are intended for cutting nail-embedded wood. Blades with many tiny teeth make cuts in metal. Thin blades are more flexible, but thick blades provide more control and straighter cuts. Wide blades are stronger but can't make cuts with tight curves. Narrow blades easily cut contours.

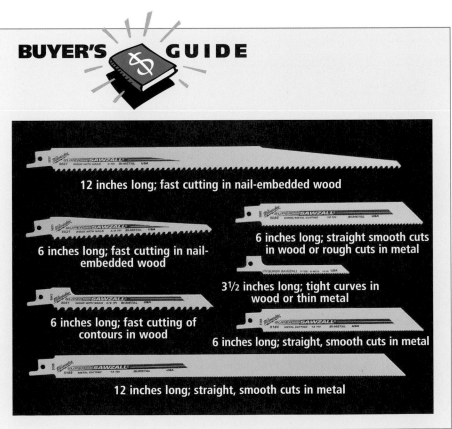

12 inches long; fast cutting in nail-embedded wood

6 inches long; fast cutting in nail-embedded wood

6 inches long; straight smooth cuts in wood or rough cuts in metal

3½ inches long; tight curves in wood or thin metal

6 inches long; fast cutting of contours in wood

6 inches long; straight, smooth cuts in metal

12 inches long; straight, smooth cuts in metal

2 FOUR DECK PROJECTS

Each of the four deck building projects featured in this chapter represents a distinct deck building style. Examine all four projects as you think about the deck you want to build. You will see how each deck is assembled, why material choices were made, and the approximate time it takes to do the work. Use this chapter to help you plan your deck. Once you determine the style and features you want, turn to the step-by-step projects throughout the rest of the book to learn all of the skills necessary to build the deck you want.

BUILDING A SINGLE-LEVEL RAISED DECK

BATTERBOARDS AND MASON'S STRING LINES are used here to lay out footing locations for a deck that is 24 feet long and 14 feet wide. A 2×12 ledger board was first attached to the house to establish the deck position. The deck structure, including number of footings, is designed to be enclosed as a four-season porch in the near future. Approximate time for a novice (with a helper) to lay out footing locations for this deck: 12–14 hours. Time includes removing siding and attaching the ledger.

HOLES FOR SEVEN 12-inch-diameter footings were dug. A standard single-level raised deck would only need four, parallel to the house. The extra footings are necessary on this deck to handle the additional weight of the roof and future remodeling project structures. Holes are 48 inches deep to get below the local frost line. The bottom of the center footing in the row parallel to the house is flared to 24 inches. The remaining footings are flared to 18 inches. Footings were dug with a power auger. Forty-four 60-pound bags of ready-mix concrete were mixed in a portable power mixer. Post anchors for 6×6 posts were installed and aligned after the concrete cured for 48 hours. Approximate time (not including curing time): 14–16 hours.

6×6 POSTS were plumbed and temporarily braced in place. Post tops were trimmed to the proper height after posts were positioned. Trimming lines level with the bottom of the ledger were established using a water level. The beam supported by the posts will have joists attached to its inner face. Approximate time: 6–7 hours.

A 24-FOOT-LONG BEAM made of doubled 2×12s was built in place on top of the row of posts parallel to the house. Adjustable post caps attach the beam to the tops of the posts. This beam serves as the header joist because joists will be attached to its inner face. The two rim joists also are beams on this deck because of the future remodeling. They will help carry the weight of the roof. The extra beams are 14 feet long and also were built in place. The remaining length of visible ledger will support the landing at the top end of the stairs. The end of the adjacent 14-foot beam is attached to the ledger with a double joist hanger. Approximate time: 7–8 hours.

14-FOOT-LONG 2×12 JOISTS were installed. The large size of the framing on this deck accommodates the future remodeling. Joist hangers attach joists to the ledger and beam header joist. Blocking pieces were fastened between joists in the middle of the span to prevent twisting of the joists. Most of the temporary bracing was removed after joists were installed. Approximate time: 8–9 hours.

BLOCKING

5/4×6 DECKING was attached perpendicular to the joists and fastened with deck screws. No additional blocking was necessary because seams between boards were centered over joists. The seams were staggered between adjacent rows of decking for best appearance. Approximate time: 7–8 hours.

BUILDING A SINGLE-LEVEL RAISED DECK (CONTINUED)

FOOTINGS FOR STAIR LANDINGS and pad were located after the main deck platform was built. Locating stair footings is more accurate when done relative to an existing deck structure. One 12-inch-diameter footing was made for a 6×6 post that will support the upper landing. Four 8-inch-diameter footings were made for 4×4 posts that will support a small transition landing in the stair run. The stair run makes a 90-degree turn at the landing to end on the 4×4-foot pad. The pad is 4 inches thick. Thirty-two 60-pound bags of concrete were mixed in a portable power mixer. Approximate time (including making a form for the pad): 6–7 hours.

POST ANCHORS were attached to the footings. Posts were plumbed and the framing for the landings installed. Decking was attached to the joists. **Note: The landing could be replaced by another deck level on a multilevel deck if desired (see Building a Multilevel Deck project, page 35–36). Calculations for the stair runs were checked and the stringers for the stairs were made.** The upper and lower stair runs were built in place. Approximate time: 16–18 hours.

You may want to add corner bracing to a deck like this for greater stability.

RAILING POST LOCATIONS were calculated and the railing posts installed. Posts were notched and attached to the outside of the perimeter framing and stringers. The two posts at the bottom end of the upper stair run are longer than other posts because they also serve as posts for adjoining railings. This saved the time and money of installing two additional posts. Approximate time: 12–14 hours.

Total approximate time for this deck: 88–101 hours.

BUILDING A MULTILEVEL DECK

SIDING WAS REMOVED and ledger boards attached to the house. The ledger boards establish the upper-deck level that will be 28 feet long by 15 feet wide. This upper level fits into an inner corner of the house. Batterboards and mason's string lines were used to locate footing positions for both levels of the deck. Approximate time for a novice (with a helper) to lay out footing locations for this deck: 15–17 hours, which includes removing siding and attaching the ledger.

THIRTEEN 12-INCH-DIAMETER FOOTING HOLES were dug. Each hole is 48 inches deep to get below the local frost line. The bottoms of the holes didn't need flaring, but tube forms were required. Concrete was delivered by truck and pumped through a hose to each footing location. Post anchors for 6×6 posts were attached to the footings after the concrete cured for 48 hours. Large footings and posts allowed for the fewest number possible for a multilevel deck of this size. Approximate time: 16–18 hours.

6×6 POSTS were installed and temporarily braced in position. A water level was used to establish post heights for each level. Posts were then trimmed at the correct height. Beams made from doubled 2×12s will sit on the posts. Joists will be cantilevered over beams on both deck levels. The lower deck level is 28 feet by 16 feet. Approximate time: 9–11 hours.

BEAMS WERE BUILT in place and attached to the post tops with adjustable post caps. The long beams were made longer than required and will be trimmed flush with the rim joists after the joists are installed. The short beam supports the upper-deck level joists that attach at the patio door bay. The bay framing isn't strong enough to anchor a standard ledger board. Beams were covered with self-sealing membrane for extra moisture protection. Approximate time: 10–12 hours.

A LEDGER for the lower-deck level was attached to the posts beneath the middle beam. The ledger sits in notches cut in the posts. Then a 2×12 header joist and rim joists were installed for both deck levels. Forty-five degree corners were made on the lower level where stairs to ground level will be built. Beam ends were trimmed flush with the rim joists. The inner 2×12 joists were attached with blocking in the middle of the joist spans on both levels. Approximate time: 19–21 hours.

⁵⁄₄×6 DECKING was installed perpendicular to the joists on the upper level. Decking was installed at opposite diagonals on the lower level. Deck screws were used to fasten the decking. The different decking patterns provide visual texture and separate the two levels. A double joist was installed at the center of the lower level to properly support the decking. Approximate time: 16–18 hours.

LOCATIONS WERE ESTABLISHED for 8-inch-diameter footings at the bottom ends of the stairs. One side of each stair run rests on a preexisting concrete slab. Only one additional footing was necessary for each stair run. Stair runs were calculated and stringers made, and the stairs were built. Each stair run ends on a low-level deck platform (see Building a Low-Level Deck, pages 37–38). A simple box stair connects the two deck levels. The levels could be farther apart and connected by longer stair runs. Approximate time (not including the low-level platforms): 12–14 hours.

RAILING POST LOCATIONS were calculated and the posts installed. Posts were notched and attached to the outside of the perimeter framing and the stringers. Coated metal tubes are used as balusters for this railing. Approximate time: 19–21 hours.

Total approximate time for this multilevel deck: 116–132 hours.

BUILDING A LOW-LEVEL DECK

FOOTING POSITIONS were established around the concrete pad surrounding a pool. The low-level deck on each side of the pool is 30 feet long and 8 feet wide; 2×8 framing will be used on this low-level deck. Smaller-dimension framing requires more footings. Batterboards and mason's string lines were used to locate footing positions. Approximate time for a novice (with a helper) to lay out footing locations for each side of the deck: 7–9 hours.

TEN HOLES for 8-inch-diameter footings for each deck side were dug with a power auger. Each hole is 48 inches deep to get below the local frost line. Tube forms were required for the footings. Concrete was delivered by truck and pumped to the footing locations. Post anchors for 4×4 posts were installed after the concrete cured for 48 hours. Approximate time (for each side): 10–12 hours.

4×4 POSTS were plumbed and temporarily braced in position. A water level was used to establish post heights, and each post was trimmed to accurate length. The ground slopes away from the concrete pad so the outer posts are longer than the inner posts. Landscape rock was added to cover the area after posts were installed, but before framing was completed. Approximate time (for each side, not including ground cover): 7–9 hours.

DOUBLE 2×8 BEAMS were built in place on top of the posts. They are attached to the posts with adjustable post caps. A 45-degree beam was installed in each corner. Decking will be attached around the deck perpendicular to the joists. The diagonal beam will support joists meeting from both directions. Approximate time (for one side, including a 45-degree beam): 10–12 hours.

2×8 RIM JOISTS and inner joists were installed. Inner joists were attached to the 45-degree beam with 45-degree joist hangers. Approximate time (for one side): 14–16 hours.

A LEDGER AND FRAMING for a box stair were installed. The front edge of the stair rests on the concrete pad. A 45-degree header joist was installed between box-stair sections in each deck corner. Approximate time (for one side, including the stair framing in a corner): 12–14 hours.

5/4×6 DECKING was installed on the deck and the box stair perpendicular to the joists. Seams between boards were staggered between adjacent rows of decking. The board ends meeting in the corner are mitered at 45-degree angles. Decking was fastened with deck screws. Approximate time (for one side, including decking on one side of a corner): 6–8 hours.

RAILING POST LOCATIONS were calculated and posts installed. Posts were notched and attached to the outside of the perimeter framing. One post was notched to fit around each deck corner. Stair railings were not needed. Coated metal tubes were used as railing balusters. Approximate time for one side, including corner post: 7–8 hours.

Total approximate time for one side: 73–88 hours.

BUILDING A GROUND-LEVEL DECK

BATTERBOARDS AND MASON'S STRING lines were used to lay out footing locations for a deck that is approximately 8 feet wide and 10 feet long. Six holes for 8-inch-diameter footings were dug with a posthole digger. Each hole is 12 inches deep. There is no frost line to deal with since this is a freestanding deck. Tube forms were used to level the footings about 1 inch above ground level. Approximate time for a novice (with a helper) to lay out footing locations, dig holes, and level tube forms for this deck: 5–7 hours.

SIX 60-POUND BAGS of ready-mix concrete were mixed in a wheelbarrow. Post anchors for 4×4 posts were attached to the footings after the concrete cured for 48 hours. The anchors were aligned with a long straight board. Diagonal measurements were checked to square the anchor positions. Approximate time (not including curing time): 3–4 hours.

BEAMS WERE MADE from double 2×6s. They were attached in the post anchors. A 1/2-inch-thick pressure-treated shim was installed between the beam and one side of the anchor at each footing. The anchor is 3 1/2 inches wide and the beam is 3 inches thick. Approximate time: 2–3 hours.

BEAM ALIGNMENT was checked and adjusted as necessary to make certain beams were square. Approximate time: 1/2–3/4 hour.

2×6 RIM JOISTS were attached to the ends of the beams. Angle brackets were installed to provide additional support for the corner joints. Approximate time: 1–1½ hours.

INNER 2×6 JOISTS were attached to the beam faces with joist hangers. Approximate time: 3–5 hours.

2×6 DECKING was installed perpendicular to the joists. Decking was fastened with deck screws. Ends of boards hang over edge of deck and will be trimmed to length after installation. Approximate time: 1½–2 hours.

A CHALK LINE was snapped to mark a straight cutting line. Decking was trimmed to length with a circular saw. Approximate time: ¼–½ hour.

Total approximate time for this ground-level deck: 16–24 hours.

LAYING OUT A DECK

Be sure that all of the elements of your deck fit together as smoothly and easily as possible by doing careful layout work. Take your time and follow your design plan. The effort will pay off with a deck that looks professional and withstands activity. Inaccurate layouts can cause problems throughout the project and can result in quality compromises.

Once you begin the layout, make the project area a kids- and dogs-free zone. Although batterboards, strings, and spikes make a tempting playground, for the safety of all concerned, make the work site off-limits.

Attaching a ledger board to the house is the first step in basic deck layout. Then batterboards and mason's string lines are used to establish footing locations. If there is an existing ledger on your house, check to see that it is flashed and attached properly (see pages 46, 185).

CHAPTER THREE PROJECTS

INSTALLING LEDGER BOARDS

LAYING OUT A DECK

Attaching the ledger to the house is the first step in laying out a deck (unless you build a freestanding deck, page 61). With this method, your deck height is established at the place where the deck attaches to the house. Install the ledger so the surface of the installed decking will be at least 1 inch below the interior floor level to keep water from seeping into the house.

Make certain the structural members of the house are sound before attaching a ledger. Framing underneath a bay window usually requires additional support to secure a ledger. Check an existing ledger and the sheathing beneath it carefully (see page 45).

Remove metal or vinyl siding so the ledger can be attached flush to the house sheathing. Cut metal siding with a metal-cutting blade (page 28) in the circular saw. Cut vinyl siding with a carbide-tipped combination blade used to cut wood.

Before installing the ledger board, look through the following pages to see what kind of installation your type of house siding requires. Also decide whether you'll need lag screws, carriage bolts, or both to attach the ledger (page 46). Then check local code requirements for the fastener spacing pattern.

SKILL SCALE

EASY **MEDIUM** HARD

SKILLS: Cutting siding, flashing, and lumber, drilling holes, driving fasteners.

HOW LONG WILL IT TAKE?

PROJECT: Installing a 16-foot ledger, installing flashing, and reattaching siding.

EXPERIENCED	3 HR.
HANDY	4 HR.
NOVICE	5 HR.

✔ STUFF YOU'LL NEED

TOOLS: Hammer, tape measure, chalk line, speed square, circular saw, level, drill, tin snips, caulk gun, ratchet and socket.

MATERIALS: Lumber, building paper, fasteners, flashing, caulk.

CUTAWAY VIEW

LEDGER BOARD ON METAL OR VINYL SIDING. Remove a section of the siding material before attaching the ledger. You may need to use a zip tool (see Tool Tip, page 43). Attach the ledger using lag screws or carriage bolts (see page 16) to the band joist or other house structure framing members.

INSTALLING LEDGER BOARDS ON METAL OR VINYL SIDING

1 **MARK LOCATIONS FOR TOP AND BOTTOM EDGES** of the ledger. The surface of the decking must be at least 1 inch beneath the interior floor surface so add 1 inch to the thickness of the deck boards you use to determine the location of the top edge of the ledger. Measure from the bottom of a door threshold to accurately determine the ledger position.

2 **REMOVE AN EXISTING LEDGER** (as on this project) that doesn't meet your project needs. Mark the new ledger position. Check for damaged sheathing or framing members after removing the ledger, especially if the ledger was water damaged (see page 45).

TOOL TIP

UNLOCKING SIDING JOINTS

Unlocking the joint between siding pieces usually requires the use of a specialty siding tool, called a zip tool. This will help prevent damage to siding pieces and allow you to get at the nails used to attach the top flange of each siding piece to the house. Insert the zip tool in the joint between two pieces (below left) and slide it down the length of the pieces, releasing the hooked edge of the top piece from the nailed flange on the bottom piece. Do this at both top and bottom joints to remove a full piece of siding (below right). Use this method to remove vinyl siding for cutting as an alternative to cutting it in place. Replace the siding after cutting it to fit around the ledger.

3 **MARK THE LENGTH OF THE LEDGER LOCATION**, adding 1½ inches at each end of the ledger position to allow for rim joist boards that will be installed later (see page 110). Add more length at each end to accommodate fascia boards if they are part of your project. Snap lines for the ledger position between the location marks you made.

4 **CHECK THE LINES FOR LEVEL**—don't assume the siding is installed level. A water level (see page 24) is helpful for long ledger areas. Adjust and remark as necessary, keeping the decking surface below the interior floor by at least 1 inch.

5 **SET THE CIRCULAR SAW BLADE DEPTH** to cut through the siding (use a blade appropriate for the siding material, see page 28) but not the sheathing underneath. Cut on the outside of the lines on the top and sides of the cutout, stopping the blade when it touches the corners. This provides extra clearance for installing the flashing and ledger. Cut about ½ inch above the bottom line, leaving a small lip of siding that the ledger will cover when installed. You also can cut vinyl siding with a utility knife and straightedge.

Always wear safety glasses and hearing protection when using a circular saw.

SAFETY ALERT!

BALANCE WHEN CUTTING
When cutting with a power saw while standing on a ladder, make sure you are securely balanced on the ladder. Don't overreach; move the ladder frequently so you are well balanced, or use scaffolding (see page 101).

6 **USE TIN SNIPS** to complete the cuts in the corners on metal siding, or use a hammer and chisel, or razorblade knife, on vinyl siding.

7 **PLACE BUILDING PAPER OVER THE SHEATHING,** sliding it underneath the siding around the perimeter of the cutout, using a few roofing nails or staples to hold it in place.

8 **CUT THE LEDGER** from lumber that is as straight as possible. Mark joist locations on the ledger, crown side on top. Mark locations now to prevent problems when attaching the ledger to the house (Step 11), but don't attach joist hangers yet (page 109).

Homer's Hindsight

FLASHING PREVENTS WATER DAMAGE
Always install flashing over the ledger so it fits up underneath the siding. I didn't on this deck and although the ledger board shows only a little water damage (near right), look what a mess (far right) I had to fix behind the board! I had to replace sheathing and framing members—much more time and money than simply installing flashing in the first place.

9 **INSERT GALVANIZED FLASHING** (often called Z-flashing) so at least 1 inch fits behind the siding. Don't pierce the flashing with fasteners—pressure should keep it in place until you install the ledger. Overlap pieces of flashing by 3 inches. Be sure to extend flashing over the full length of the cutout area, so it will cover rim joists and fascia. You may need to notch the flashing to fit around door thresholds. Cut flashing with tin snips.

10 **RAISE THE LEDGER INTO POSITION** and drive one nail at the center top edge of the board. Level the board and the ledger in place with nails in the upper corners. Reinstall cut siding pieces along the bottom of the ledger, if necessary, as on this project. Slide the upper edge of the siding underneath the ledger before driving the fastners in the next step.

  WORK SMARTER

CARRIAGE BOLTS OR LAG SCREWS?

A carriage bolt (top) requires a through hole and access to the space behind the band joist to attach and tighten the washer and nut. A carriage bolt provides a more secure connection and is preferred if access is available, but lag screws (bottom) are a perfectly acceptable alternate fastener. Use carriage bolts wherever you can, but don't be concerned about using lag screws in other places. A lag screw requires only a pilot hole and can be driven into the band joist or any other framing member from outside the house. The attachment pattern will usually be specified by local code. Decks supporting heavy loads should have pairs of fasteners installed every 16 inches, otherwise install one fastener every 24 to 32 inches, alternating between the top and bottom of the ledger.

11 **MARK FASTENER LOCATIONS** for attaching the ledger (see Work Smarter, left). Center fasteners about 2 inches from board edges. Don't install fasteners near joist locations; they interfere with joist hangers or make joist installation more difficult.

12 **DRILL PILOT HOLES** and install the fasteners. Lag screws should be long enough (usually 4¹/₂ inches) to penetrate the sheathing and at least 1¹/₂ inches into framing members. Tighten each screw until the washer begins to compress the wood underneath. After installing all the screws, go back and check each one, retightening as necessary. Wait about 24 hours for the ledger to settle in position and retighten the screws.

13 **USE CARRIAGE BOLTS** that are at least 5 inches long to allow room for the washer and nut from the back side of the band joist (inside the house). After installation, check and retighten as with lag screws in Step 12.

14 **APPLY SILICONE CAULK** to the seam between the flashing and the siding and between the ledger and the siding along the bottom edge. Add flashing if there is a big gap along the bottom edge of the ledger. Install the rim joists (or fascia) before caulking the seams at the ends of the ledger.

15 **CUT NOTCHES FOR OBSTACLES** such as vents or hose bibs (see page 132 for how to make an access panel for a hose bib). On a notch for a vent, cut an angled bottom edge using a reciprocating saw or jigsaw so airflow isn't restricted.

INSTALLING LEDGER BOARDS ON WOOD SIDING

Attaching a ledger to a house with wood siding is similar to attaching a ledger to a house with metal or vinyl siding. Determine and mark the ledger position based on the design plan. Make sure you keep the ledger at least 1 inch beneath the interior floor and follow the basic methods shown on pages 43–44.

Unlike metal and vinyl siding, you may have difficulty when you try to slide the flashing behind the wood siding remaining above the ledger position. Depending on where you've made the ledger cutout, the flashing may be blocked by nails attaching the remaining siding to the house framing before the flashing is fully inserted. Cut V-notches into the flashing at these spots to position it properly—at least 1 inch of the flashing must extend behind the siding.

SKILL SCALE

EASY   **MEDIUM**   HARD

SKILLS: Cutting siding, flashing, and lumber, drilling holes, driving fasteners.

HOW LONG WILL IT TAKE?

PROJECT: Installing a 16-foot ledger, installing flashing, and reattaching siding.

EXPERIENCED . . . . . 3 HR.

HANDY . . . . 4 HR.

NOVICE . . . . 5 HR.

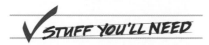

✓ STUFF YOU'LL NEED

TOOLS: Hammer, tape measure, chalk line, speed square, circular saw, level, drill, tin snips, caulk gun, ratchet and socket.

MATERIALS: Lumber, building paper, fasteners, flashing, caulk.

CUTAWAY VIEW

LEDGER BOARD ON WOOD SIDING A section of wood lap siding must be cut and removed to attach the ledger flush to the band joist or other framing members. The ledger will crush siding and make a weak connection if installed over it. Install flashing behind the siding above the ledger, making a watertight seal protecting both the ledger and the house framing.

1 **CUT THE SIDING** after marking the ledger position and cutting lines (see pages 43–44). Set the circular saw depth to cut through the wood siding and not the sheathing underneath. Cut on the outside of all the lines, including the bottom side of the ledger position. Stop each cut when the saw blade touches the corner. Use a hammer and sharp wood chisel to finish the cuts in the corners. Use a pry bar to remove the waste pieces of siding. Remove all remaining nails and debris.

2 **INSTALL THE LEDGER** after sliding galvanized flashing behind the wood siding at the top of the ledger space. At least 1 inch of the top flashing flange must fit behind the siding. You may have to trim the flashing to fit around a door threshold or around nails attaching the siding to the house. Put the ledger in place. Level it and tack it in place. Drill pilot holes and install the fasteners, either carriage bolts or lag screws (page 16). Apply caulk at the top and bottom seams. Caulk the end seams after rim joists and fascia are installed.

A+ WORK SMARTER

MAKING A LONG LEDGER

If you need a longer ledger than you can make from one board, cut two (or more) boards to fit. Each board must be at least 3 feet long. Butt the boards together. If mounting a ledger to vertical framing members, such as wall studs, rather than the house band joist, the splice between boards must be centered on a framing member. Since you can't use lag screws at the splice, drill pilot holes and drive nails or screws on both sides of the splice into the framing member. Most local codes also require additional support from a mechanical fastener, such as a strapping plate, at the splice (page 18).

49

INSTALLING LEDGER BOARDS ON STUCCO

Siding material usually isn't removed to attach a ledger board to stucco. Also, building paper isn't used. The upper flange on the flashing is bent to fit into a shallow cut made in the stucco surface. The cut is made and the flashing installed after the ledger board is attached to the house. To make this work the heads of the fasteners must be sunk below the surface of the ledger (see below). Otherwise the ledger is positioned and attached using the basic methods used with metal and vinyl siding. Extend the flashing beyond the ends of the board to cover rim joists and fascia.

Some local codes require that flashing be installed behind the stucco surface. This is a complicated job that you should leave to a professional contractor.

To install the ledger board as flat as possible against the wall, flatten large ridges or bumps in the stucco surface within the outlined ledger board position. Install pairs of fasteners every 16 inches to keep the ledger flat on uneven surfaces.

SKILL SCALE

EASY | **MEDIUM** | HARD

SKILLS: Cutting stucco, flashing, and lumber, drilling holes, driving fasteners.

HOW LONG WILL IT TAKE?

PROJECT: Installing a 16-foot ledger and flashing.

EXPERIENCED	3 HR.
HANDY	4 HR.
NOVICE	5 HR.

✔ STUFF YOU'LL NEED

TOOLS: Hammer, tape measure, speed square, circular saw, level, drill, tin snips, caulk gun, ratchet and socket.

MATERIALS: Lumber, fasteners, flashing, caulk.

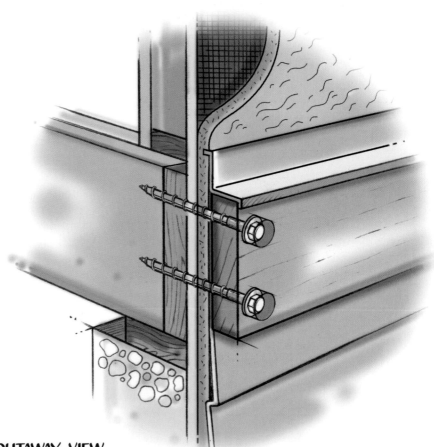

CUTAWAY VIEW

DRILL A COUNTERSUNK HOLE wide and deep enough so the washer and head of each fastener will be below the ledger surface. This is necessary so the fasteners won't interfere with a circular saw used to cut a kerf in the stucco. Drill pilot holes through the centers of the countersunk holes and install the fasteners. You may want to use a masonry bit to cut through the stucco layer (usually less than 1 inch thick) after drilling through the ledger with a regular twist bit. Stucco can chew up a twist bit quickly. Switch back to a twist bit to complete the pilot hole in the framing member.

WORK SMARTER

GOOD HELP WHEN YOU NEED IT

It's easier to have a helper when attaching a ledger to a house, but if you must work by yourself, use braces. Use braces even when you have a helper when attaching a ledger to masonry surfaces. Lean braces of scrap lengths of lumber against the house at an angle so they can support the ledger board. Lift the ledger onto the braces, then adjust each brace by moving the bottom end closer or farther from the wall until the ledger is level. Leave the braces in place until you attach both ends of the ledger to the wall.

1 **MAKE A ³⁄₈-INCH-DEEP CUT** (a kerf) in the stucco using a masonry blade. First mark the ledger position, then brace and level the ledger board in place. Mark fastener locations, drill countersunk pilot holes (see opposite), and install the fasteners. Measure the height of the top flange on the galvanized flashing. Subtract ¹⁄₄ inch from this measurement and mark a line at this distance above the top edge of the ledger. Attach a straight piece of 1× stock to the ledger as a cutting guide.

2 **APPLY SILICONE CAULK** to the kerf, or flashing, seam. First use pliers to bend a ¹⁄₄-inch lip in the top edge of the flashing. This doesn't have to be a perfect bend—just make it as straight and even as you can. The flashing and kerf allow for slightly imperfect measurements. Place the lip of the flashing in the kerf and position the flashing on the ledger. Press on the flashing all along the length until it seats firmly on the ledger and in the kerf. Then apply the silicone caulk. Also fill the countersunk holes with caulk.

INSTALLING LEDGER BOARDS ON MASONRY

A ledger mounted on concrete requires flashing. Once you install the ledger board, cut and install flashing to extend beyond the board ends enough to cover rim joists and fascia. Caulking the seam between ledger and wall doesn't provide enough protection. Masonry anchoring sleeves are an option to epoxied threaded rods for attaching the ledger.

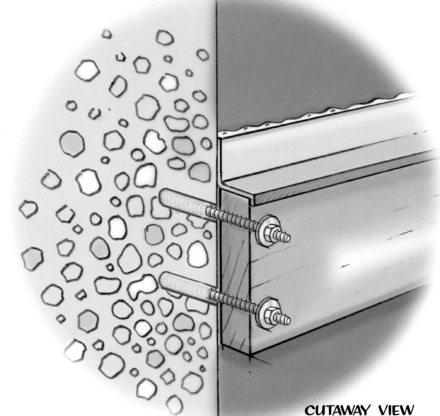

CUTAWAY VIEW

LEDGER BOARD ON MASONRY Attaching a ledger to concrete is simple when using threaded rods, secured with epoxy, into holes drilled into the concrete wall. Since the rod requires the same diameter hole in the ledger and the wall, both holes are drilled after bracing the ledger into position.

EASY	MEDIUM	HARD

SKILLS: Cutting lumber and flashing, drilling holes in concrete, driving fasteners.

HOW LONG WILL IT TAKE?

PROJECT: Installing a 16-foot ledger and flashing.

EXPERIENCED	3 HR.
HANDY	4 HR.
NOVICE	5 HR.

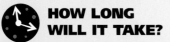

✔ STUFF YOU'LL NEED

TOOLS: Hammer, tape measure, speed square, circular saw, level, hammer drill, tin snips, caulk gun, ratchet and socket.

MATERIALS: Lumber, fasteners, epoxy, flashing, caulk.

KNOW WHERE FASTENERS GO
Fasteners should penetrate a concrete block wall in the mortar joints (the seams between blocks) or in the webs (the solid portions of each block that surround the hollow core areas, called voids). Plan fastener positions for the mortar joints and adjust the ledger position if necessary unless you are confident of the web position (position depends on the type of concrete block used in the wall). Check local code regulations because there are different standards for where fasteners should be placed.

1 **MARK A LEVEL OUTLINE** of the ledger position on the concrete surface (this project is on concrete block). Because wall surface material isn't cut and removed, you don't need to allow extra space for the rim joists or fascia. You will install flashing to cover these (Step 8).

2 **BRACE THE LEDGER BOARD** firmly to drill through it and into the wall behind it. First mark the joist locations on the ledger board, then raise and brace it into position (see Work Smarter Tip on page 51). Make sure it is level, adjusting the braces if necessary.

3 **DRILL PILOT HOLES** through the board using a twist bit. Mark fastener positions for pairs of fasteners every 16 inches (see Tip on page 54).

4 **CHANGE TO A MASONRY BIT** the same diameter as the twist bit. Insert the bit through the hole in the ledger and drill a 3-inch-deep hole into the wall.

LAYING OUT A DECK

5 **USE A SHOP VACUUM** to remove debris from the holes. You may find it helpful to use a bottle brush or other narrow object to loosen the debris while vacuuming.

DON'T SCRIMP ON HARDWARE

I didn't see any reason why the same 12p nails I'd used for years on other building projects weren't good enough for attaching a ledger for a small deck. When a friend asked me if the 2-inch gap he saw between the ledger and house was supposed to be there, I knew the nails weren't right. Fortunately my mistake was only expensive and not disastrous, because I took the deck apart and attached the ledger properly—before the deck collapsed while my friends and I were standing on it.

6 **AFTER PREPARING THE EPOXY SYRINGE** (see page 16) following the manufacturer's instructions, insert the syringe tip into a hole and squeeze out the recommended amount. (One syringe usually contains enough epoxy for 6 holes.) Always wear gloves while handling epoxy—and follow the manufacturer's safety recommendations.

7 **QUICKLY INSERT A THREADED ROD** into the hole after applying the epoxy. You have only a few minutes before it begins to harden. Let the epoxy harden completely (usually for 24 hours, depending on weather conditions), following manufacturer's directions.

8 **INSTALL A WASHER AND NUT** on each rod and tighten until the washer compresses the wood underneath. Check the bolts after 24 hours and retighten if necessary. Apply a heavy bead of silicone caulk in the corner at the top edge of the ledger and the concrete, and seat the galvanized flashing into it. When the flashing is firmly embedded in the caulk, apply more caulk to the seam along the top edge of the flashing.

THE CARPENTER'S TRIANGLE

The key part of a typical deck layout is making certain the deck will be square to the house and that the sides of the deck will be square to each other. An out-of-square layout causes problems all through the building project: footings in wrong spots, skewed posts and beams, joists of uneven lengths, and uneven decking patterns. That said, don't fret if your 18-foot deck is ¼ inch off. No one will know, unless you tell them.

Make a squared layout by establishing right angles (90 degrees) at the corners. Although a framing square forms a right angle, it is too small to accurately establish squared layout lines of the lengths needed for a deck project.

Use simple geometry known as the "3-4-5 carpenter's triangle." A triangle with sides that measure 3, 4, and 5 feet has a right angle in the corner where the 3- and 4-foot sides meet. Multiples of 3-4-5 also work, such as 6-8-10, 9-12-15 or 12-16-20. (Use any unit of measure with the 3-4-5 triangle, such as inches, yards, or metric units, but feet usually work best for deck layout.) Get the best accuracy by using the largest triangle possible. Make reference marks at correct distances on mason's string using marked pieces of masking tape.

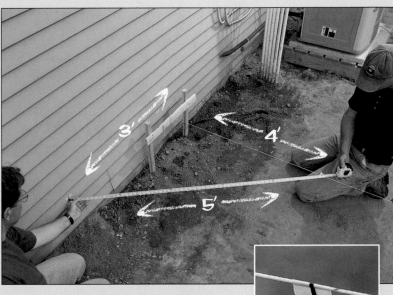

MEASURE AND MARK 3 FEET along the house or ledger from the corner you establish. (A piece of marked masking tape works well on siding.) Measure and place a piece of marked masking tape on the mason's string (inset) so the mark is at 4 feet. Place the hook end of a tape measure at the mark on the wall and measure diagonally to the mark on the string. Adjust the position of the string on the batterboard opposite the wall until this measurement is exactly 5 feet.

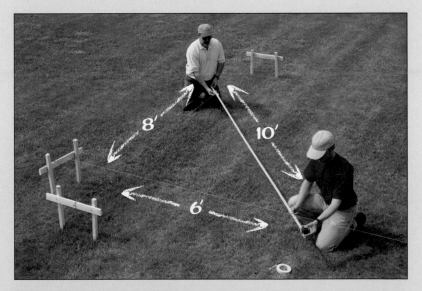

FOR A FREESTANDING DECK, first establish a string line on batterboards that represents one side of the deck. Make another set of batterboards and mason's string so the two strings intersect at the corner location. Measure and place a piece of marked tape on the first string at a multiple of 3 (here we used 6 feet). Measure from the corner and place marked tape at 8 feet on the second string. The distance between the marks should be 10 feet. Move the second string opposite the corner to adjust as necessary.

LAYING OUT FOOTING LOCATIONS

LAYING OUT A DECK

After the ledger is in place, determine locations for footings that support the posts. Accurate layout work depends on tightly stretched string lines. Mason's string is very strong, can be stretched tightly without breaking, and won't relax and sag later. Don't use a substitute. Batterboards must be rigid to withstand the pressure from tightly pulled lines so use stakes long enough to be driven securely into the ground.

SKILL SCALE

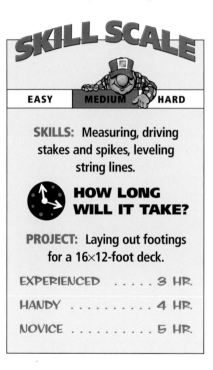

EASY	MEDIUM	HARD

SKILLS: Measuring, driving stakes and spikes, leveling string lines.

HOW LONG WILL IT TAKE?

PROJECT: Laying out footings for a 16×12-foot deck.

EXPERIENCED	. . . . . 3 HR.
HANDY	. . . . 4 HR.
NOVICE	. . . . 5 HR.

✓ STUFF YOU'LL NEED

TOOLS: Tape measure, maul, tripod, plumb bob, line level, mason's string.

MATERIALS: Lumber, screws, spikes, masking tape, colored marking tape.

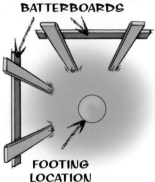

BATTERBOARDS

FOOTING LOCATION

LAY OUT BATTERBOARD. Batterboards make a stable base to support the mason's string that forms the layout lines. Each batterboard is made of two stakes and a crosspiece made from 2×2, 2×4, or 1×4 lumber. Sharpen the ends of the stakes, which must be long enough to be driven firmly into the ground, to support tightly stretched mason's string. Attach the crosspiece to the stakes with screws. Batterboards no taller than 3 feet work best.

1 MARK THE CENTER of the outside post location on the ledger. Drive a screw or nail at the bottom edge of the ledger, leaving enough of the fastener as a tie-off point for a layout string.

A+ WORK SMARTER

LEVEL YOUR LINE LEVEL

Position a line level within 12 inches of the end of a line for greatest accuracy. Although it weighs very little, placing the line level toward the middle of the string can affect the level of the string, especially when the string is longer than 20 feet. A water level (see page 24) may be more accurate for leveling batterboards across long distances.

2 **DROP A PLUMB LINE** from the center mark made in Step 1 if you have a ledger higher than 3 feet from the ground, as in this project. You'll work with batterboards and layout lines closer to the ground.

3 **DRIVE IN A BATTERBOARD** near the wall at the bottom of the plumb line so the crosspiece is level. If the ground slopes away from the house, install the crosspiece close enough to the ground so the batterboard at the opposite end of the string will be no more than 3 feet high. Make a mark on the crosspiece aligned with the plumb line. Tie one end of the mason's string to a screw driven into the wood near the mark. Wrap the string several times around the crosspiece and align it with the mark on the last wrap.

ACCURATE PLUMB LINES

Drop an accurate plumb line using the right tools. Although a chalk line can be used as a plumb bob (top photo, left), it is cumbersome to use and easily affected by wind. A solid metal plumb bob (top photo, right) is easy to use, and its small profile and weight make wind less of a problem. Use a camera tripod or similar object to make a plumb line support (bottom photo). To drop accurate plumb lines:

Keep plumb lines about ⅛ inch away from layout lines (inset). To get an accurate position, do not allow string lines to touch.

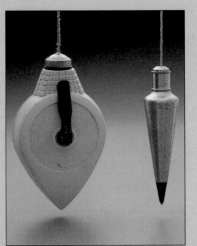

LAYING OUT FOOTING LOCATIONS (CONTINUED)

FRAMING SQUARE

4 **YOU ALSO CAN ATTACH THE BATTERBOARD** crosspiece to a wall, using deck screws on wood siding or self-tapping masonry screws on concrete walls. (Don't do this on vinyl or metal siding.) Use this method when you can't drive stakes close to the wall. (When you remove the crosspiece, fill the small holes left in the wall surface with caulk.)

5 **POSITION THE BATTERBOARD** for the opposite end of the mason's string using a tape measure and framing square. Place the framing square corner at the center mark on the wall (or ledger) with the short leg of the square against the wall. Place the hook end of a tape measure at the wall and corner of the framing square, align the tape with the long leg of the square and measure out about 2 feet past the footing location. Drive stakes for the batterboard without attaching the crosspiece.

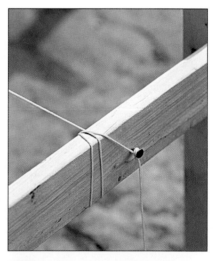

6 **START SCREWS** to attach the crosspiece to the stakes and one near the middle to anchor the string. Hold the crosspiece against the stakes, stretch the string until it is tight, and wrap it several times around the crosspiece. Tie the string to the anchoring screw, leaving at least 12 inches free. Place a line level on the string, then adjust the position of the crosspiece until it is level. Finish driving the screws.

7 **STRETCH THE STRING TIGHTLY** (it won't break). Retie if necessary. Use the carpenter's triangle (see page 55) to make a right angle between the string and the wall. Adjust the position of the string at the batterboard opposite the house.

8 **MARK THE CROSSPIECE** on the second batterboard where the string crosses the top edge, once you've created a square corner. This provides a reference point to ensure the string hasn't moved (in case it gets jostled) and for adjustments to the string position you may need to make when checking the completed deck layout.

9 **MARK THE CENTER POSITION** for the outside post at the other end of the ledger. Make a squared layout line with batterboards and mason's string following the steps for the first line. If you plumb down from a high ledger, measure down from the ledger and level the crosspiece for the batterboard nearest the house at the same height as that on the first set of batterboards.

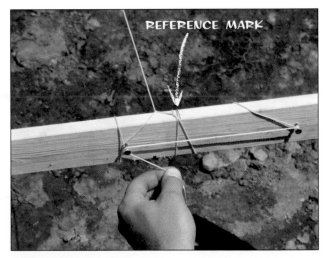

REFERENCE MARK

10 **MEASURE OUT FROM THE HOUSE** and mark the distance for the footing locations on both layout lines. Make another set of batterboards and mason's string parallel to the ledger with the leveled string crossing the first layout lines at the footing location marks. Level this last string about ⅛ inch above the other strings: Strings that touch as they cross affect the accuracy of the layout lines. After making this last layout line, measure the diagonals of the rectangle formed by the strings. The measurements should be equal.

11 **MEASUREMENTS OFTEN AREN'T EQUAL**—First check all measurements and string positions, rechecking for square with the 3-4-5 triangle, and adjust if necessary. Then remeasure the diagonals. If the measurements still aren't equal, adjust the string ends of the first two layout lines at the batterboards opposite the house until they are equal. Loop the free end of a string across the stretched portion and pull it to move the string—use the reference mark made earlier on the crosspiece to gauge how much. Tie the string end to another screw if necessary.

LAYING OUT FOOTING LOCATIONS (CONTINUED)

12 **MEASURE AND MARK THE LAYOUT LINES** for the footing positions between the intersecting lines that mark the corner footing positions. First make sure the layout lines are square. For this project three footings lie parallel to the ledger between the corner footings, and one footing is centered between the ledger and each of the two corner footings.

13 **DROP A PLUMB LINE** at each footing location to locate the center of the footing location on the ground. Position a spike (at least 12 inches long) at this spot and drive it into the ground as straight as possible. Tie a piece of colored marking tape or similar material to each spike to make them visible. If wind disturbs the plumb line, use a piece of plywood as a windscreen.

OPTION: Mark footing locations for a beam that is at a 45-degree angle to other framing members after creating the basic squared layout lines. Measure and mark equal distances from the intersection of the squared lines on each string line. Install batterboards and mason's string for the angled beam so the string crosses the other layout lines at the marks. Measure and mark along this angled line and drop a plumb line to locate the footings.

14 **MAKE A "STORY POLE"** (a marking template) from a straight piece of 1×4 or strip of plywood a little over 4 feet long. Along one edge, mark the center point and 24 inches on both sides of the center point. Position the story pole so the center mark is aligned with a spike at the center of a footing position. Drive another flagged spike at each of the 24-inch marks, keeping the spikes as vertical as possible. Make sure that the spikes are in a straight line when you drive the third spike.

15 **USE THE STORY POLE** to position and drive spikes for the remaining post locations. These spikes will be reference points for relocating the center of each footing after the holes are dug and the concrete poured.

LAYING OUT A FREESTANDING DECK

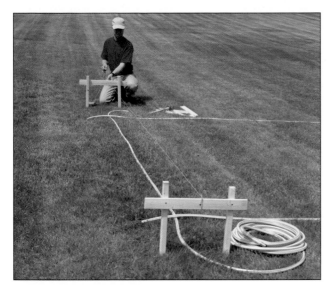

1 **USE A GARDEN HOSE** or similar method to determine the rough position for a freestanding deck. Choose a side of the deck that will be perpendicular to the joist direction (usually one of the long sides). Make a layout line of batterboards and mason's string at the center of the footing positions along this side, which will serve as the ledger side of the deck layout.

2 **DETERMINE THE CENTER** of the outside corner footing position. Make another set of batterboards and mason's string for a layout line perpendicular to the first layout line that stretches at least 18 inches beyond the footing locations at the other side of the deck. Use the 3-4-5-triangle method to make certain this line is at a right angle to the first line.

3 **MAKE A SECOND LAYOUT LINE** perpendicular to the first ledger layout line at the center of the other outside corner footing positions. Measure and mark the two perpendicular layout lines for the centers of the footings opposite the ledger line. Make a layout line that crosses these marks. Measure the diagonals and adjust the string ends opposite the ledger line until the layout lines are square to each other.

Homer's Hindsight

MEASURE TWICE, DIG ONCE
A valuable carpentry rule is: "Measure twice, cut once." Well, "Measure twice, dig once" is equally valuable for deck building. I didn't recheck my measurements even though I plumbed for footings the day after I established the basic string layout. A batterboard must have shifted or a string been bumped because I ended up with a few footings in the wrong places. Digging and pouring new footings wasn't fun, believe me. Before I ever dig footings again, I'll save some backbreaking extra labor by checking the layout—at least twice!

4 DIGGING & POURING FOOTINGS

Solid, level footings establish a solid, level deck. Have the number, locations, and size of the footings for your deck plan (page 11) approved by a building inspector before you begin to dig. Call to have all underground utilities marked before you dig. Use caution when digging near the marks—they're not always exactly accurate. Most local codes require an inspection of the footing holes before concrete is poured. Schedule delivery of ready-mix concrete after you're confident of the inspection date.

FOOTINGS

CLOSER LOOK

FOOTING REGULATIONS

Footing regulations established by local codes are based on ground conditions in the area. The depth and construction method for deck footings depends on whether an area has a frost line and the type of soil and slope of the ground at each project site. Before digging, check with local building officials for the required hole depth and diameter. If the deck will be near a pond or marshy area, footings may need to be larger than normal to adequately support the deck.

A typical footing (top, right) is a round hole filled with concrete. The diameter and depth of the hole is determined by local code. Footing depth will be below the frost line in cold climate areas. The frost line is the depth in the ground beneath which the ground doesn't freeze. Freezing and thawing cycles in the soil cause ground movement above the frost line. This movement can shift portions of the deck structure and cause major structural problems. Footings must extend beneath the frost line to prevent this damage. You also may be required to flare the bottom of the hole. Making the footing bottom wider than the top prevents movement of the footing in the ground. A layer of compactible gravel (usually 3-6 inches thick) frequently is required in the bottom of the hole to drain water away from the base of the footing. The hole can be dug in firm ground with the ground serving as the form. A concrete tube form may be required in loose soil to prevent the hole from collapsing before concrete is poured. The form also keeps moisture in the curing concrete from being absorbed too quickly by the surrounding soil, which weakens the concrete.

Footings in areas without frost lines (bottom, left) are often square and shallow (2×2 feet and 1 foot deep are common). This type usually doesn't require a separate form. If one is necessary, cover the sides of the hole with pieces of treated plywood. Some areas don't require in-ground footings—precast concrete footings are set directly on level ground (page 75).

The bottom of a footing must be "7 feet from daylight" at the incline on sloping ground (bottom, right). On steep slopes this requires deep holes that are difficult to dig. When working on a steep slope, hire a professional to install footings and frame the deck.

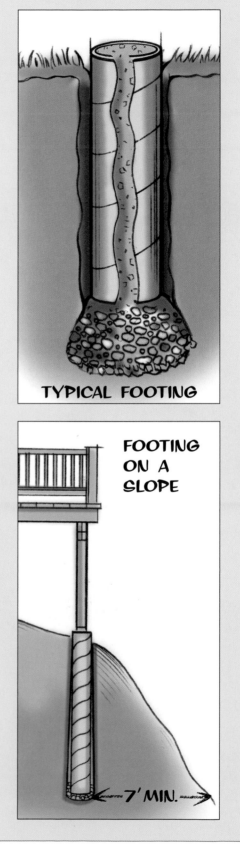

TYPICAL FOOTING

FOOTING ON A SLOPE

7' MIN.

FROST-FREE FOOTING

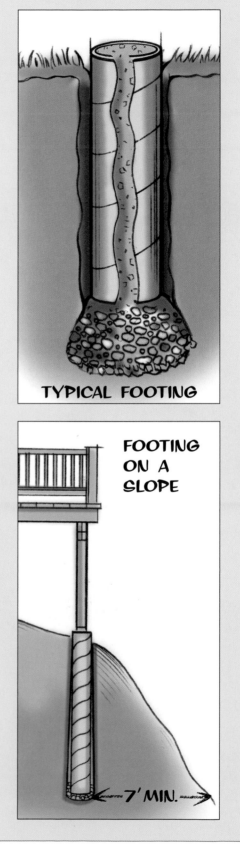

FOOTINGS

DIGGING FOOTINGS

igging footing holes by hand with either a post-hole digger or a hand auger is quick and inexpensive if you need only a few shallow holes. Rent a gas-powered auger when you have many deep holes to dig. These tools dig with large auger bits available in common footing diameters (usually 8 inches, 10 inches, and 12 inches). A trailer hitch is necessary to tow the one-person machine home. The machine is counterweighted to raise the heavy, dirt-laden bit out of the hole. A two-person gas-powered auger is less expensive to rent and is easier to move around, but it is less powerful and you must lift the bit out of the hole without assistance from the machine. The two-person auger is very useful for flaring the bottoms of holes. Otherwise you have to do it by hand. Either of these power machines should have a safety switch that stops the motor when the switch is released.

If you hit rocks or roots, don't try to power through. Back out the auger and check to see what's obstructing the hole. Many rocks can be pried out with a pinch or pry bar. If you hit a rock ledge, check local codes to determine whether you can use concrete bonding adhesive, then pour concrete on top.

The footing holes for the project shown here were dug with a one-person gas-powered auger. Each hole is lined with a concrete tube form and is 12 inches in diameter, 48 inches deep, flared, with a 4-inch layer of compactible gravel at the bottom.

BEFORE YOU DIG HOLES, check with local utilities to make certain no underground cables or pipes exist where you will dig. Also move any sprinkler-system pipes or low-voltage landscape lighting wires that may be in the way.

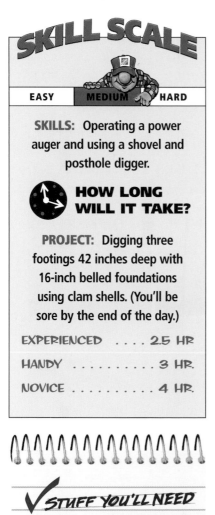

SKILL SCALE

EASY — MEDIUM — HARD

SKILLS: Operating a power auger and using a shovel and posthole digger.

HOW LONG WILL IT TAKE?

PROJECT: Digging three footings 42 inches deep with 16-inch belled foundations using clam shells. (You'll be sore by the end of the day.)

EXPERIENCED	2.5 HR
HANDY	3 HR.
NOVICE	4 HR.

✔ **STUFF YOU'LL NEED**

TOOLS: Power auger, shovel, posthole digger, maul, level, handsaw, tamper.

MATERIALS: Concrete tube form, lumber, compactible gravel.

ONE-PERSON GAS AUGER

TWO-PERSON GAS AUGER

HAND AUGER

POSTHOLE DIGGER

1 **DIG A FOOTING HOLE** at each footing location. Remove the middle reference spike at the footing location and center the bit over this spot. Do not disturb the other spikes or batterboards. Raise the bit frequently as it turns to clear dirt from the hole.

2 **ATTACH A BIT EXTENSION** to a smaller-diameter bit used to flare the bottom of the hole. Use a two-person auger to cut the flare. An extension also is used when digging the main hole if you need a deeper hole than the bit alone can dig. If you use a two-person auger, attach the extension whenever it will make it easier to lift the bit out of the hole.

3 **ROCK THE AUGER** in a circular motion while the bit turns. Keep the tip of the bit at the bottom of the hole to remove dirt at the bottom of the hole sides to make the hole flared. Also use a posthole digger to flare the hole. In both cases, a posthole digger is useful to remove the last loose dirt from the hole.

WORK SMARTER

EASY DIRT REMOVAL

Pile dirt removed from footing holes on plastic sheeting when working on grass to make it easier to haul away excess dirt without damaging the grass. Don't leave the loaded plastic down too long in hot weather—the grass may wilt within a day.

4 **TAMP A LAYER** of compactible gravel of the code-required thickness (usually 3–6 inches) at the bottom of the hole. Use a piece of post or a heavy tool made with flattened ends, a tamper (shown), to compact the gravel.

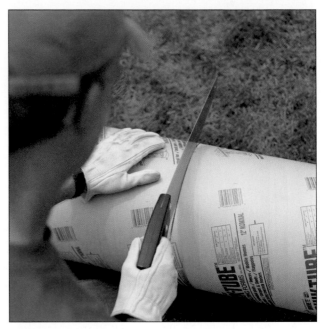

5 **CUT A CONCRETE TUBE FORM** with a handsaw or reciprocating saw. Measure the tube length so the top will be 1–2 inches above ground level and the bottom will be near the point where the flared sides begin. Make a few measurement marks around the tube and stretch a piece of string around the tube aligned with the marks. Use the string to guide your pencil to scribe the cutting line.

6 **INSERT THE TUBE FORM** into the footing hole. Twist the form as if it were a screw to push it into the hole. A tight fit is fine, but don't crush the form by forcing it—shave dirt from the sides of the hole until the form fits snugly.

7 **LEVEL THE TOP** of the tube form. This will make the top of the footing level when the form is filled with concrete. Level the form in all directions. A level footing makes installing posts and beams easier.

8 **BRACE THE TUBE** in place, if necessary, to make certain it stays level. In loose soils the sides of the hole may collapse while you dig or after the hole is dug (another good reason to use forms). If the form is loose within the hole, make certain it is centered according to the reference spikes before bracing.

9 **BACKFILL AROUND THE FORM** but don't tamp the dirt too much. This may distort the shape or position of the form. If the footing hole is significantly larger than the form, wait to backfill until you've poured concrete into the form. Otherwise dirt will fill the flared portion of the hole.

USING A POSTHOLE DIGGER

A posthole digger is handy even if you dig footing holes with a gas-powered auger. Use it to remove loose dirt that an auger can't lift from the bottom of a hole. The posthole digger also can be used to flare a footing hole, and it's an option when you have a few shallow holes to dig. Push the handles together (top right) to spread the blades before ramming it into the dirt. Pull the handles apart (center), forcing the blades together to capture loose dirt. Keep the handles spread to bring dirt out of the hole. Open the blades to dump the dirt. Keep a piece of scrap wood handy to bang the blades against so you can knock off soil that sticks.

Another option when digging a few shallow holes: Twist a hand auger (bottom) to dig the fixed blades into the ground. Periodically dump dirt that collects inside the blades.

DIGGING FOOTINGS FOR A GROUND-LEVEL DECK

The tops of the footings for a ground-level deck must be level with each other and about 1 inch above ground. Framing for a ground-level deck is made from 2×6 lumber that sits directly on the footings, without posts (page 39). The surface of the decking is one step up from ground level. Ground-level decks should be built on ground that is fairly level. You may need to grade the site to make the deck level at the right height above the ground.

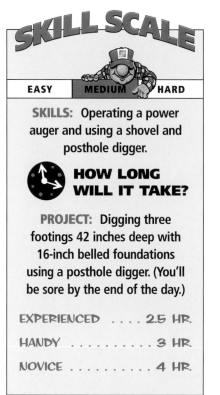

SKILL SCALE

EASY   **MEDIUM**   HARD

SKILLS: Operating a power auger and using a shovel and posthole digger.

HOW LONG WILL IT TAKE?

PROJECT: Digging three footings 42 inches deep with 16-inch belled foundations using a posthole digger. (You'll be sore by the end of the day.)

EXPERIENCED . . . . 2.5 HR.

HANDY . . . . 3 HR.

NOVICE . . . . 4 HR.

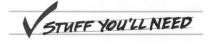

STUFF YOU'LL NEED

TOOLS: Power auger, shovel, posthole digger, maul, level, handsaw, tamper.

MATERIALS: Concrete tube form, lumber, compactible gravel.

1 RESET THE BATTERBOARD CROSSPIECES and mason's string lines (pages 56-60) after locating footing positions and digging holes as you would for a typical deck. The bottom edges of the crosspieces should be level with each other and about 1 inch off the ground. Tie mason's string to extend from the bottom edges of the crosspieces and to align with the outside edges of the holes.

2 LEVEL CONCRETE TUBE FORMS inserted in the holes so the tops align with the mason's string lines. Use forms even if they're not required by local code. They are the easiest way to make footings with tops that are level with each other. Pour concrete as for other footings (following pages).

POURING FOOTINGS

Concrete is caustic; use caution when working with it. Wear eye protection, dust mask, and long clothing. Avoid dropping bags of cement and creating a dust cloud. Before you purchase bags of cement, consider how much concrete you'll need and how sore you'll be at the end of the day. One bag of dry cement weighs 60 pounds. Multiple that by the number of bags you need, then add water weight. It's probably worth a little additional expense to have premixed concrete delivered and poured.

If you decide to mix it yourself, add water to the dry ingredients: sand, portland cement, and gravel aggregate. Buy the ingredients in the correct proportions premixed, available in 60- or 90-pound bags.

Mix the ingredients by hand in a wheelbarrow with a square-tipped shovel or use a specialty tool called a mortar hoe, which resembles a large garden hoe with two big holes in the blade. The shovel mixes well, it will be used to help place concrete in holes, and you probably already own one. Rent either an electric- or gas-powered mixer if you must mix concrete for several footings (Tool Tip on page 71). Or have the cement delivered.

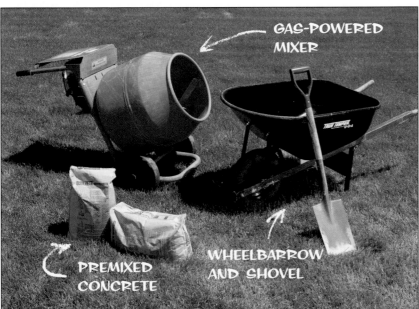

GAS-POWERED MIXER

PREMIXED CONCRETE

WHEELBARROW AND SHOVEL

FOOTINGS

WORK SMARTER

THE SIMPLEST MIXING METHOD
For a large number of footings have ready-mixed concrete delivered by a commercial concrete supplier. Specify that the concrete will be used for deck footings and how much you need (page 12). The contractor will provide the proper concrete mix to your site. (Many suppliers set a minimum purchase.) Make sure you have the holes approved by the inspector before scheduling the concrete delivery. The supplier will want to dump the load quickly. Have several friends lined up with wheelbarrows to carry the mixed concrete from the truck and dump it into the footing holes. Check how much time you'll have from the time the truck arrives. Keep in mind that the driver will not help you unload or fill holes! Most concrete suppliers also provide the option of pumping the concrete from the delivery truck through a hose (right) directly to the holes. The ease and time savings of this option are usually well worth the extra cost over standard delivery rates.

MIXING CONCRETE

Concrete must be mixed to the correct consistency for strength and durability. If you've never mixed concrete, buy an extra bag and practice the mixing technique. Wear eye protection whenever you work with concrete. Measure and note the amount of water you use to make a correct mix. This amount will be the same whether you mix in a wheelbarrow (below) or in a power mixer. Check with a building inspector to determine whether concrete mix must be tested for proper consistency.

Before you start mixing by hand, consider how much concrete you need. It might be worth hiring a truck to pump ready-mix concrete into the footing holes. If you decide to mix it yourself, you can rent a power mixer rather than mixing by hand.

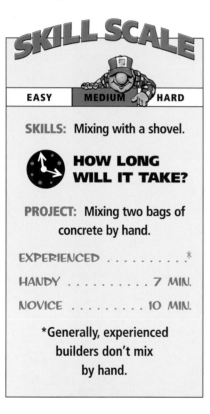

SKILL SCALE

EASY   MEDIUM   HARD

SKILLS: Mixing with a shovel.

HOW LONG WILL IT TAKE?

PROJECT: Mixing two bags of concrete by hand.

EXPERIENCED . . . .*

HANDY . . . . 7 MIN.

NOVICE . . . . 10 MIN.

*Generally, experienced builders don't mix by hand.

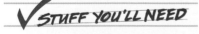

STUFF YOU'LL NEED

TOOLS: Wheelbarrow, shovel, trowel.

MATERIALS: Premixed concrete, drinkable water.

1 MIX CONCRETE IN A LARGE WHEELBARROW. Empty a bag of premixed ingredients into the wheelbarrow. **(NOTE: Never use a partial bag of premixed concrete because it won't have the correct proportion of ingredients.)** Pour about one-half gallon of clean water into a depression made in the mound of ingredients. Begin mixing by moving dry material from the sides of the mound into the water-filled depression. Work carefully so you don't slop water out of the wheelbarrow, which will remove some of the ingredients necessary for a proper mix.

2 MIX THOROUGHLY until the water combines with the dry ingredients. If the mixture is still dry and crumbly, add a small amount of water, less than 1 cup, and continue mixing.

3 **TEST THE MIX** by scooping up some on a trowel. Concrete mix of the proper consistency holds its shape, and no water is visible. Continue adding increasingly smaller amounts of water and mixing until the mix is just right.

4 **A RUNNY MIX** means there is too much water. Add another bag of premix if there is room in the wheelbarrow to mix it well. Combine the new ingredients thoroughly with the runny batch before adding more water—it may not be needed. Test and mix as necessary until the batch reaches the proper consistency.

TOOL TIP

POWER MIXING SAVES TIME AND MUSCLES

Mixing concrete in a wheelbarrow is fine when you only have a few shallow footings to fill. Each 60-lb. bag of premixed concrete makes 1/2 cubic foot of concrete—enough to fill about 9 inches of a 12 inch-diameter tube form. Rent a power mixer to make your work much easier if mixing more than a dozen bags. (See page 12 for concrete estimating guidelines.) The type shown here is portable; the concrete can be mixed and poured at each footing location.

Make certain you understand how to safely operate the power mixer before leaving the rental center. (An electric power mixer should be plugged into a GFCI-protected outlet or extension cord.) Never reach hands or tools into the mixer while it is operating. Stop the mixer to check the mix consistency.

Mix each batch of concrete to the proper consistency. Each batch will take a few minutes. After dumping the previous batch, pour about 1/3 of the premix and half the water for the next batch into the mixer. Run it for a minute to gather residue from the previous batch before adding the remaining materials and finishing the new batch.

POURING CONCRETE

Pouring concrete is hard work. Think about how many footing holes you need to fill. If your deck requires six 40-inch holes, you will pour enough concrete to fill a 20-foot hole! (Consider having premix concrete pumped into the holes.)

There are several things that must be done to the concrete before it hardens. A helper or two will be very useful, especially if you pour many footings. Always pour a complete footing. If you need to mix another batch of concrete to finish filling a hole, do so before the first batch dries. If you're using a mixer, place it next to the footing holes before adding the ingredients to the mixer.

Working wet concrete after it is poured requires a few special techniques. Screeding (opposite page) makes a flat, level surface on all footing types. Floating, edging, and other techniques used on pad footings are shown on pages 80-81.

Attach a post anchor to a footing after the footings cure (harden) for a few days. This method is shown on page 88. Methods for installing fasteners while the concrete is wet are shown on page 74.

FOOTINGS

SKILL SCALE

EASY   MEDIUM   HARD

SKILLS: Mixing, pouring, and screeding concrete.

HOW LONG WILL IT TAKE?

PROJECT: Pouring concrete, screeding, and inserting J-bolt for one footing.

EXPERIENCED . . . . *

HANDY . . . . 45 MIN.

NOVICE . . . . 1 HR.

*An experienced builder will usually have the footings poured.

STUFF YOU'LL NEED

TOOLS: Power mixer, shovel.

MATERIALS: Premixed concrete, lumber.

SAVED BY BATTERBOARDS

I have big feet and don't pay proper attention. I must have dislodged a couple of reference spikes sometime while digging the footing holes and pouring concrete. I learned why it is a good idea to keep the batterboards in place. I retied the mason's string lines at the reference marks on the crosspieces and accurately replumbed for the footing centers without wasting too much time.

1 **USE A SHOVEL** to guide concrete into the footing hole. This type of power mixer allows you to mix at the footing and pour directly from the mixer into the hole. You can pour from a wheelbarrow if that's where you mix the concrete. Some concrete may slop outside the form, but don't scrape it up and put it into the footing—dirt weakens the mix.

2 **PLUNGE A LENGTH OF SCRAP WOOD** into the concrete when the footing is almost full. Work it up and down within the footing to eliminate air pockets. On footings deeper than 2 feet, do this when the footing is half full and again when full.

3 **REMOVE EXCESS CONCRETE** with a length of 2×4 to level the top of the footing after overfilling the form slightly. Push the 2×4 back and forth in a sawing motion as you move it across the footing to screed the concrete surface. If you insert fasteners into the wet concrete, see the variations on the following pages. If not, go right to Step 4.

4 **LET THE CONCRETE IN THE FOOTINGS CURE** for about 48 hours. In hot weather, especially in direct sun, mist the concrete occasionally so the concrete surface doesn't cure too quickly, which may make it brittle and cause it to deteriorate. If it is hot, cover the footings with clear plastic sheeting after misting so they will cure properly.

REINFORCE FOOTINGS

Local codes may require reinforcing footings with rebar (page 76). This is common on footing columns that are several feet above ground level. Cut pieces of rebar about 4 inches shorter than the depth of the footing. Insert the rebar into wet concrete after screeding the surface. Each piece should be at least 2 inches from the footing form with its top end pushed at least 3 inches below the concrete surface. Add concrete and smooth as necessary.

73

POST ANCHOR FASTENERS

FOOTINGS

J-BOLTS

1 **INSERT THE HOOK END** of a J-bolt into wet concrete after screeding. Use the story pole and reference spikes to position the bolt at the center of the footing location established during the deck layout. The J bolt may be slightly off center in the concrete footing.

2 **LEAVE ¾–1 INCH OF THE THREADED END** above the concrete surface. Use a speed square to determine whether the bolt end is vertical. Add concrete and smooth as necessary for a flat footing surface. Let the concrete cure (page 73). Then attach an adjustable post anchor (page 90).

WET-INSERT POST ANCHOR

1 **INSERT THE FINS** of a wet-insert post anchor (also known as a post anchor with concrete fins) into wet, screed concrete. Use a story pole to position the anchor accurately in the footing. Wiggle the anchor slightly as you push the fins into the concrete. This type of anchor doesn't require bolts and may be required by local code.

2 **USE A LONG STRAIGHTEDGE** (or story pole) to align post anchors to each other. Work with a helper if you have several footings. This type of post anchor is more difficult to install because of the extra alignment necessary while the concrete is still wet. Let the concrete cure (page 73).

A+ WORK SMARTER

LINE 'EM UP
You must be accurate when placing wet-insert anchors because they can't be moved once the concrete cures. Place a board inside the anchors to make sure they line up before the concrete sets.

PRECAST CONCRETE PIERS

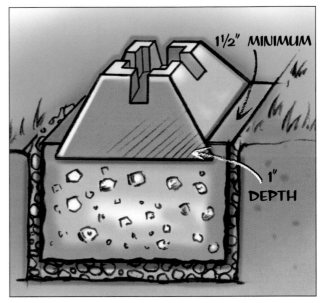

1½" MINIMUM

1" DEPTH

1 **SOAK PRECAST CONCRETE PIERS** in water for a few minutes before using. Dry piers draw moisture away from the concrete in the footing and weaken the bond between them. Precast concrete piers are usually used on square footings level with the ground. The square recesses formed in the piers support posts. The rectangular grooves support 2× lumber (such as rim joists) on edge.

2 **ALIGN THE PIER** on the footing after screeding the concrete surface. The footing should be at least 1½ inches wider than the pier on each side. Push the pier about 1 inch into the concrete. Make certain the top of the pier remains level. Smooth the footing surface and let the concrete cure (page 73). Bolt a metal post anchor to the pier (below left).

PRECAST CONCRETE PIER OPTION: Precast piers also can be used when footings aren't required by local code. The pier is placed directly on level, firm ground (though code may require a layer of compactible gravel underneath it). Bolt a metal post anchor to the pier (page 88) even if not required by local code; the anchor securely fastens a post to the pier.

Homer's Hindsight

DON'T TRUST HISTORY
My neighbor down the street built a deck about five years ago and had his work approved by a building inspector. I wanted to build a similar deck, so I talked with him about how he did his footings. I went ahead and dug my footings based on the information he gave me. I had the time available and figured I could get my plan approved later. Big mistake! Local code regulations had changed since my neighbor built his deck. I muttered, "Approval first, then dig," all the way back to the rental center.

75

POURING PAD FOOTINGS

Pad footings are usually rectangular. Forms contain the poured concrete until it cures. (Leave curved forms to professional contractors.) Pads support heavy items, such as spas or brick barbecues, better than deck structures can. Pads are often built above ground level to position the unit at the proper height to the deck. Make a pad at least 3 inches wider on each side than the base of the heavy item resting on it. Ground-level pads often support the bottom of stair stringers.

The ground-level pad project on pages 77–81 shows installing a 4×4-foot pad at the foot of stairs. Four-inch-thick concrete is poured over a 4-inch-thick layer of compactible gravel. Local code for this project didn't require extra reinforcement of the pad. The raised-level pad project, pages 82–86, will support a spa. The top of the pad is 16 inches higher than the ground, to place the top of the spa at the right height for a 4-foot-high deck (see page 86). The pad is 4 feet by 4 feet (the base of the spa is 3 feet 6 inches by 3 feet 6 inches).

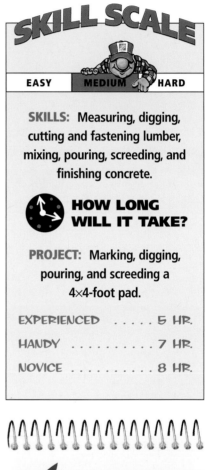

SKILL SCALE

EASY · MEDIUM · HARD

SKILLS: Measuring, digging, cutting and fastening lumber, mixing, pouring, screeding, and finishing concrete.

HOW LONG WILL IT TAKE?

PROJECT: Marking, digging, pouring, and screeding a 4×4-foot pad.

EXPERIENCED	5 HR.
HANDY	7 HR.
NOVICE	8 HR.

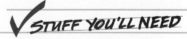

✓ STUFF YOU'LL NEED

TOOLS: Tape measure, shovel, tamper, circular saw, drill, hammer, level, power mixer, masonry finishing tools.

MATERIALS: Lumber, compactible gravel, premixed concrete, 3-mil plastic sheeting.

SPECIAL MATERIALS are often required by local codes when pouring pad footings. The concrete pad may require reinforcement to prevent cracking. For large concrete pads, #10 wire mesh is often used. It comes in flat sheets, often 3 feet by 3 feet, or in long rolls that are 4 feet wide. Cut it to size with tin snips. Rebar is a steel reinforcing bar also known as reinforcing rod. Pieces of rebar are fastened together in a grid for pads (or used individually in column footings). Fasten pieces of mesh or rebar together with 18-gauge wire. Bolsters center pieces of mesh or rebar within the pad thickness before pouring concrete.

POURING A GROUND-LEVEL PAD

1 **MARK THE OUTLINE** on the ground of the area to be removed for the pad. First lay out the pad excavation area with batterboards and mason's string (pages 56–60). This area should be at least 1½ inches wider on each side than the finished pad size to allow for 2×4 forms. After marking the outline (flour works well) take down the mason's string.

WORK SMARTER

CUTTING REBAR

Rebar is tough stuff—your arm will wear out before you finish cutting one piece with a hacksaw. Use a metal-cutting blade (page 30) in a reciprocating saw. Clamp the rebar to a piece of wood and keep the saw-foot plate against the rebar while cutting to reduce vibration.

FOOTINGS

TOOL TIP

CONCRETE TOOLS FINISH THE JOB

Inexpensive concrete tools will contribute to a professional-looking concrete pad. A small pointing trowel is used to separate the concrete from the form. (It also is handy to test proper consistency of the concrete mix, page 71). A margin trowel is a general-purpose trowel used in small areas or corners. A float creates a smooth surface on concrete. A metal float makes a hard, smooth finish. Texture the surface of a stair pad (page 81) to provide safe traction if you use a metal float. A wood float leaves a slightly rougher surface than the metal float, but adding additional texture to a stair pad is a good idea. Use an edger to smooth and shape corners at the edges of a pad.

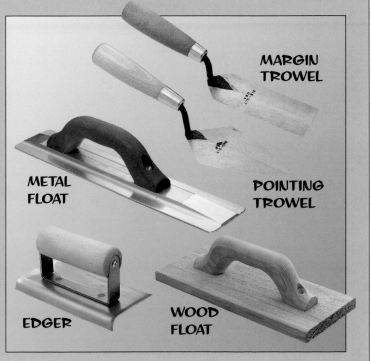

MARGIN TROWEL

METAL FLOAT

POINTING TROWEL

EDGER

WOOD FLOAT

2 **REMOVE GROUND** from the excavation area, following the marked outline. Plan for a 4-inch layer of compactible gravel and a 4-inch-thick concrete pad, with the surface of the pad 1 to 2 inches higher than soil level. (Adjust thicknesses to meet local code specifications if necessary.) Level the bottom of the excavation as much as possible.

3 **POSITION A 2×4 FORM AND DRIVE STAKES** on the outside of the form. The length of the 2×4 should be equal to the length of the pad plus 3 inches (so it will overlap the adjacent form pieces). Make 1-foot-long stakes from 1×3 lumber. Drive them about 6 inches from the ends of the form. Retie the string line to help position the 2×4 if necessary.

4 **LEVEL THE FORM BOARD** at the correct height. Attach it to the stakes with screws driven through the stakes and into the 2×4. Use a reciprocating saw to remove the top of a stake that is higher than the top edge of the form.

5 **INSTALL THE OPPOSITE 2×4 FORM PIECE** so it is level with the first piece. This second piece should be the same length as the first. Attach it to stakes parallel to the first form piece. Place the level on a straight piece of lumber if the distance between form pieces is greater than the length of the level.

6 **DRIVE SCREWS** through the first two form pieces into the ends of the remaining 2×4 form pieces. The length of these pieces is equal to the width of the pad. Square the form by measuring the diagonals and adjusting as necessary until they are equal. Make sure the form is level. Attach the last two form pieces to stakes driven near the ends.

7 **TAMP A LAYER** of compactible gravel of the code-required thickness over the ground. Make this as level as possible so the correct thickness of concrete can be poured. Position reinforcement (page 76) over the gravel if required (local code didn't require reinforcement for this pad). Coat the inside of the form with vegetable oil for easy form removal.

8 **PLUNGE A SCRAP** piece of lumber into the concrete in various spots to settle the concrete and to remove air pockets. Don't disturb reinforcement. Add more concrete until the form is slightly overfilled.

9 **SCREED THE CONCRETE SURFACE.** Fill low spots with more concrete and screed again if necessary.

FOOTINGS

10 **SMOOTH, OR FLOAT, THE CONCRETE SURFACE** with a float (see Tool Tip on page 77). Float the concrete just long enough to make it smooth and to bring a thin layer of water (bleed water) to the surface. Finish floating quickly after bleed water appears.

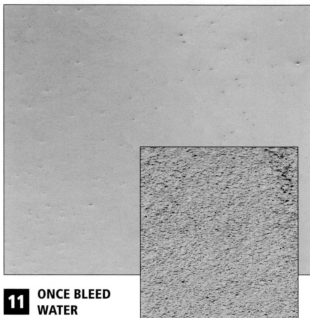

11 **ONCE BLEED WATER APPEARS,** (inset) concrete should be left alone until the water evaporates. The concrete has hardened just enough for you to finish the surface. Working concrete before bleed water disappears makes the concrete surface brittle, and brittle pad surfaces deteriorate quickly.

12 **PUSH THE POINT** of a small trowel about 1 inch into the seam between concrete and form. Cut along the seam around the pad perimeter to separate the concrete from the form.

13 **WORK AN EDGER** around the perimeter seam to smooth and shape the corner of the pad. Work the edger in either direction. Lift the leading edge slightly as you move the tool in one direction so the edge doesn't dig into the concrete.

14 **USE A STIFF BRISTLE BROOM** to add a slightly rough texture to the pad. This provides better traction for pads at the foot of stairs.

SAFE LANDING
Besides supporting the bottoms of stair stringers, a ground-level pad is a landing for frequently used stairs. It is more attractive than a worn spot in the grass and provides safer traction. Check local codes. Some may requre footings under a landing pad.

15 **COVER THE PAD** with a piece of 3-mil clear plastic sheeting. Let the pad cure for at least a week. This allows the concrete to harden properly and will protect the surface from defects. If the weather is hot, lift the plastic occasionally and mist the pad slightly with water so the surface doesn't dry too quickly.

16 **REMOVE THE FORM** after the concrete has cured. Remove the stakes before prying off the 2×4 form. Backfill the space around the pad with soil.

POURING A RAISED-LEVEL PAD

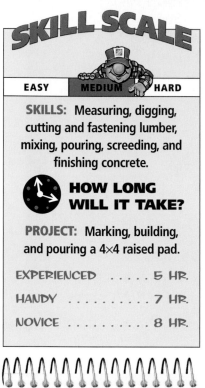
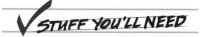

STUFF YOU'LL NEED

TOOLS: Tape measure, shovel, tamper, circular saw, drill, hammer, level, power mixer, masonry finishing tools.

MATERIALS: Lumber, compactible gravel, premixed concrete, 3-mil plastic sheeting.

A+ WORK SMARTER

A raised pad contains a large amount of concrete. The project on these pages used about 15 cubic feet—that's thirty 60-lb. bags of premixed concrete to mix by hand! Plan your project so ready-mixed concrete is delivered for the pad and deck footings at the same time.

1 **REMOVE 4 INCHES OF SOIL** from the pad area. Lay out the pad excavation area with batterboards and mason's string (see pages 56–60). This area should be about 3/4 inches wider on each side than the pad's finished size to allow for 3/4-inch plywood forms. Use flour to mark the outline of the area to be removed. Take down the mason's string before digging. The pad should be 3 inches wider on each side than the base of the unit it will support.

2 **ATTACH TWO ADJACENT SIDES** of the form with screws. Make the sides of the form from 3/4-inch plywood cut to size. One pair of sides should be 1 1/2 inches longer than the other pair. Attach the longer pieces so they overlap the shorter ones. Measure the depth of the excavation after digging and add this distance to the height needed for the form pieces.

3 **LEVEL THE TOPS** of the forms. Place the level on a straight piece of lumber if the distance between form pieces is greater than the length of the level. Place shims under the bottom edges of the plywood if necessary.

4 **MEASURE THE DIAGONALS** of the form and adjust until they are equal to square the form (page 55).

5 **ATTACH A 1-FOOT-LONG 2×4 CLEAT** on both sides of each upper corner of the form. The top edge of each cleat should be flush with the top of the plywood. Overlap one cleat over the end of the other. The overlap should be the reverse of the overlap of the plywood sides at that corner. Drive 2-inch screws through the plywood into the cleats. Drive screws through each overlapping cleat into the end of the cleat it covers.

6 **ATTACH ADDITIONAL CLEATS** every 3 feet between the corners. (The sides of the form for this project are 4 feet long. The cleats are centered between the corners.)

83

FOOTINGS

7 **DRIVE 1-FOOT-LONG STAKES** made from 1x3 lumber at the base of the form sides. Place stakes about 6 inches from each corner and every 3 feet between the corners. Drive 1½ inch screws through the stakes into the plywood. It isn't necessary to drive the stakes underneath the cleats.

8 **SHOVEL AND TAMP** a 4-inch layer of compactible gravel at the bottom of the form. Use a post or tamping tool to compact the gravel.

9 **DRIVE SCREWS** to secure the top end of a brace underneath each cleat. Cut the braces from scrap 2×4 lumber. Each brace should be long enough to span between cleat and ground at a 45-degree angle. Place one end of a brace under a cleat and drive a 1-foot-long 1×3 stake at the foot of the brace to wedge it in place.

10 **MOUND CLEAN FILL** (see Closer Look on page 85) in the form. There should be a 6-inch clearance between the fill and the sides of the form. Another 6 inches should be left between the fill and the top of the form for the horizontal portion of the pad.

11 **USE BOLSTERS** or small pieces of clean fill to position the reinforcement required by local code. (Never use pieces of wood or other material that will decompose and leave a void in the pad.) Center the reinforcement (#10 wire mesh for this project) within the thickness of the concrete but no closer than 4 inches to the sides of the form.

BUILDING A RAISED PAD

A raised pad, unlike a ground-level pad or deck footing, isn't a solid piece of concrete. It is easier and less expensive to pour a thick layer of concrete around a center area containing clean fill—material that won't deteriorate, decompose, or compress under heavy weight. Pieces of masonry, rubble, or stone make excellent clean fill. Pile the material in a mound, filling the spaces between large pieces with small pieces. A tight pile won't shift and less concrete will be needed to fill the form.

Check your local code about reinforcement and other regulations for raised pads. (Raised pads higher than 3 feet are more difficult to build and should be installed by professional contractors.) The building inspector will need to approve the form and reinforcement before concrete is poured. Plan this into your schedule.

FOOTINGS

12 **FILL THE FORM** with concrete. Ideally the concrete supplier can pump concrete to the form through a hose (page 69). Otherwise build a sturdy ramp to take wheelbarrow loads up conveniently.

85

13 **PLUNGE A PIECE** of scrap wood into the concrete around the sides of the form and pound on the outside of the form with a mallet to settle the concrete and remove air pockets. Slightly overfill the form with concrete.

14 **USE A LONG STRAIGHT 2×6** to screed the surface of the concrete (page 79). Fill low spots with more concrete and screed again. It may take several passes to remove excess concrete and leave a flat, even surface that is level with the top of the form.

15 **USE A FLOAT** to smooth the concrete surface until bleed water appears (page 80). If the pad will be visible, use an edger to shape the corners (page 80) after the water evaporates. Cover the pad with 3-mil clear plastic sheeting and cure the concrete thoroughly (page 81). Remove the form and backfill the space around its base with soil.

Designer Tip

A raised pad allows you to set a spa within your deck at exactly the height you want. Check manufacturer's specifications carefully before building the pad. Also check whether local code requires railings around the spa.

5

FRAMING

F raming, the structural support for a deck, usually consists of posts, beams, and joists. These structural pieces shape the deck and support the visible decking and railing. Pressure-treated lumber should be used so the deck framing will be a strong structure.

Metal framing connectors (see page 17) make the deck stronger, and many local codes require them. Use fasteners specified by the manufacturer when attaching connectors. The strength and holding power of metal connectors depend on the use of the correct fasteners.

The lumber used for framing is heavy. Have a helper available for projects in this chapter.

Lumber measurements are nominal (see page 9). Measure each board before attaching fasteners.

FRAMING

CHAPTER FIVE PROJECTS

ATTACHING POST ANCHORS

Installing adjustable post anchors is the easiest way to attach posts to footings. This type of post anchor allows for about ½-inch discrepancy in any direction for the location of the fastener connecting the anchor to the footing. Install threaded rod fasteners with epoxy after footings have hardened to accurately locate fasteners at the footing centers. Or use masonry anchoring sleeves to install bolts. Make sure concrete cures at least 48 hours before drilling holes to attach the post anchors. You also can insert J-bolts into wet concrete of poured footings (page 74). Temporary bracing used to hold posts vertical should be left in place until you begin to install decking boards. Page 90 shows installation of adjustable post anchors and 6×6 posts.

4×4 POST

4×6 POST

6×6 POST

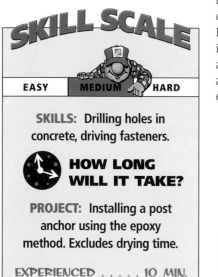

SKILL SCALE

EASY | MEDIUM | HARD

SKILLS: Drilling holes in concrete, driving fasteners.

HOW LONG WILL IT TAKE?

PROJECT: Installing a post anchor using the epoxy method. Excludes drying time.

EXPERIENCED . . . . . 10 MIN.

HANDY . . . . 15 MIN.

NOVICE . . . . 20 MIN.

✓ STUFF YOU'LL NEED

TOOLS: Hammer drill, speed square, tape measure, shop vacuum, ratchet, and socket.

MATERIALS: Threaded rod, washer, and nut, epoxy, adjustable post anchor.

1 **DRILL A HOLE** for a threaded rod that will fasten the post anchor to each footing. Use a hammer drill and an appropriate size masonry bit for the diameter of threaded rod you use (see page 16). Set the depth gauge on the drill so that ¾ to 1 inch of threaded rod will be left above the footing surface. Locate each hole position with the story pole and reference spikes. Make vertical holes, using a speed square to align the drill.

2 **REMOVE DRILLING DEBRIS** with a shop vacuum. Clean the hole thoroughly so the epoxy (see page 16) used to secure the threaded rod will firmly bond with the concrete. Use a thin object, such as a bottle brush, to help clear material from the hole.

3 **INJECT EPOXY** into the hole with the mixing syringe provided by the manufacturer. Insert a threaded rod as soon as the epoxy is injected—it begins to harden immediately. Use enough epoxy so a small amount is pushed from the hole when you insert the rod. You can remove the rod and inject more epoxy if you work quickly. Wrap a piece of masking tape around the rod to indicate the proper depth, if necessary. The tape also will keep epoxy out of the threads. One syringe contains enough epoxy for four to six holes. Wipe excess epoxy with a rag. Wear gloves to protect your skin when working with epoxy.

4 **CHECK THE HEIGHT** of the rod above the footing. Make certain the rod is fully inserted into the hole. Let the epoxy cure for 16 to 24 hours. Follow the manufacturer's directions. Curing times vary according to temperature and moisture conditions. If more than 1 inch of the rod is exposed after the epoxy cures, cut it shorter with a hacksaw or a reciprocating saw with a metal-cutting blade. Before cutting, install a nut on the rod past the cutting point. Remove the nut after cutting to rethread the cut end.

5 **PLACE A WASHER AND NUT** over each threaded rod after positioning an adjustable post anchor (see page 90) on the footing. Tighten each nut so the anchor can still be adjusted but its position isn't loose.

6 **MEASURE FROM THE HOUSE** foundation to align post anchors. Align anchors on footings parallel to the house first. Use a straight 2×4 or other long straightedge to help with alignment. Mark each anchor position on its footing with a pencil after alignment. These marks will help you gauge anchor position adjustments as well as provide a reference point if an anchor is knocked out of alignment.

7 **MEASURE THE DIAGONALS** after aligning all the post anchors. Make adjustments as necessary until the measurements are equal. This makes the post anchor positions square to each other and to the house.

WORK SMARTER

ALWAYS ADJUSTABLE

The position of an adjustable post anchor can be adjusted even after it is attached to a post, though you'll probably need a thin wrench. The post rests on the raised portion of the anchor base. Place an appropriate-size wrench in the slot and loosen the nut enough so the anchor position can be adjusted by tapping with a hammer. Retighten the nut once the anchor is repositioned.

8 **TIGHTEN EACH NUT** to secure the post anchors after squaring the alignment. Use a ratchet and appropriate-size socket to tighten the nuts. The anchor should not move, but do not tighten too much and do not strip the nut or threaded rod.

FRAMING

SETTING POSTS

osts must be plumb for your deck to be stable and so other framing members can be accurately aligned. A helper makes plumbing posts much easier. The easiest method for cutting posts to length is to do so after installing them in post anchors (see page 94).

(see page 94).

SKILL SCALE

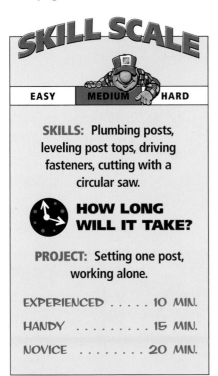

EASY   MEDIUM   HARD

SKILLS: Plumbing posts, leveling post tops, driving fasteners, cutting with a circular saw.

HOW LONG WILL IT TAKE?

PROJECT: Setting one post, working alone.

EXPERIENCED . . . . . 10 MIN.

HANDY . . . . 15 MIN.

NOVICE . . . . 20 MIN.

✓ STUFF YOU'LL NEED

TOOLS: Tape measure, speed square, hammer, drill, speed level, water level, circular saw.

MATERIALS: Lumber, fasteners, masking tape.

1 **CHECK THE ENDS** of a post for square with a speed square. If neither end is square, mark and cut one end to square. The post should be as straight as possible. Make sure the post is longer than needed if you will trim it to length after installing it on the footing.

2 **DRIVE ONE NAIL** halfway into the center hole of one post anchor flange after setting the squared post end into the post anchor. This will keep the post in the anchor and allow enough movement so the post can be installed plumb (vertical). Drive the nail only halfway so it can be repositioned if necessary.

3 **ATTACH TEMPORARY BRACING** to the post to hold it vertical. Make stakes at least 1 foot long from 1×4 or 2×2 lumber. Use 1×4 lumber for the braces. Make braces long enough to span from the ground to the top area of the post at a 45-degree angle. Attach one end of a brace to a stake with screws. Position two screws about 3 inches apart where the other end of the brace crosses the post. Drive them just until the points penetrate the back side of the brace. Plumb the post (see Tool Tip on page 92) before driving the screws into the post. Attach the other brace in the same way.

FRAMING

PLUMB POSTS WITH A SPEED LEVEL

A SPEED LEVEL makes quick work of plumbing a post. Temporarily attach it near the top of the post (masking tape or a large rubber band work well). Plumbing a post is more accurate when done near the top. Two horizontal level bubbles on the faces of the speed level allow you to plumb both directions simultaneously. The vertical level bubble isn't used to plumb posts.

4 Drive a nail into each hole in the post anchor flanges after the post is plumbed and attached to temporary bracing. Use nails specified by the anchor manufacturer. Follow Steps 1–3 for the remaining posts.

5 **OPTION A:** Mark the posts where they are level with the bottom of the ledger. A water level (see page 24) makes this job easy and accurate. For this project the posts will be cut at this mark. Because the beam will be attached to the top of the posts and joists will be attached to the inner face of the beam, the beam must be level with the ledger.

OPTION B: Measure and mark posts for decks that will have a solid decking surface with the surface sloped away from the house. Solid deck surfaces, such as plywood sheets or fiberglass coating, do not have gaps between boards. A slope is necessary for water from rain or melting snow to run away from the house. The slope should be 1 inch for every 10 feet of deck measured perpendicular to the house.

OPTION C: Subtract the width of a beam from the mark that is level with the bottom of the ledger when joists will sit on top of the beam. Adjust post height appropriately if joists will be made from lumber narrower than the ledger.

FRAMING

WORK SMARTER

CHECK IT AGAIN

Retie the mason's string lines onto the batterboards to check post alignment. Position the string so it is half the thickness of the post, plus 1/8 inch, from the footing center reference marks on the batterboard crosspiece. For the 6×6 posts in this project, this will be 2 7/8 inches from the reference mark (2 3/4 plus 1/8). The extra 1/8 inch keeps the string from resting on the post faces. Adjust post anchors or temporary bracing as necessary.

6 **USE A SPEED SQUARE** and mark a level cutting line around the post. Mark all four faces to accurately guide the saw blade when trimming a post in place (see page 94).

Be sure to coat the cut post tops with wood sealer

7 **LEVEL, MARK, AND CUT** the tops of the remaining posts. Safety Note: Make certain you have secure footing and are well balanced when trimming posts in place. Move your ladder when cutting adjacent post faces rather than trying to reach them from one position.

POST CUTTING

CUTTING POSTS BEFORE INSTALLING

CUT A 4×4 POST on a power miter saw when you're confident of the final length. This usually happens on decks where footings are made with the tops level (see page 66). Posts also are cut to length prior to installation when building railings. Adequately support the ends of the post before cutting. Posts larger than 4×4 can't be cut on a power miter saw and must be cut with a circular saw or reciprocating saw (below).

Height of the support should be equal to the height of the saw table

CUTTING POSTS AFTER INSTALLING

ADJUST THE DEPTH SETTING on your circular saw so the blade is fully extended. Cut along the scribed line on each face of a 6×6 post (above, left). This will leave a small uncut portion at the center of the post. Cut through this with a reciprocating saw (center) or handsaw. Circular saws with 7¼-inch blades will cut through a 4×4 when used on opposite faces of the post. Saws with smaller blades may require the two-step method used on 6×6 posts. Trim a post sandwiched between beam boards using a reciprocating saw with a long wood-cutting blade (above, right).

POST NOTCHING

NOTCHING ACROSS THE MIDDLE OF A POST

SKILL SCALE

EASY | MEDIUM | HARD

SKILLS: Measuring and layout, cutting lumber, smoothing with a chisel.

HOW LONG WILL IT TAKE?

PROJECT: Setting one post, working alone.

EXPERIENCED . . . . . 10 MIN.
HANDY . . . . 15 MIN.
NOVICE . . . . 20 MIN.

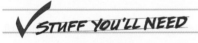

✓ STUFF YOU'LL NEED

TOOLS: Tape measure, speed square, circular saw, hammer, chisel.

MATERIALS: Lumber.

1 **CUT THE OUTSIDE BORDERS** of the notch, the shoulders, with a circular saw. Set the blade depth so it is equal to the depth of the notch. Guide the saw with a speed square so the shoulder cuts are straight and square. Mark notch locations for multiple posts using the first marked post as a template to create identical notch locations. Notching makes the face of the post flush with the outside face of the rail or beam sitting in the notch.

2 **MAKE MULTIPLE CUTS** with the circular saw between the shoulder cuts. A speed square isn't necessary because these cuts don't need to be square. The object is to make enough kerfs to leave thin wafers of post material.

3 **BREAK THE WAFERS** with a hammer. Use the hammer claws to scrape as much waste material from the notch area as you can.

4 **CUT THE REMAINING WASTE MATERIAL** from the bottom of the notch with a sharp 1-inch-wide chisel. Cut with the beveled edge of the chisel facing up. Only the notch bottom needs to be flat and smooth enough for the board to fit in it properly.

NOTCHING ACROSS A POST END

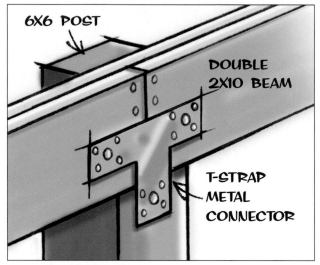

6X6 POST

DOUBLE 2X10 BEAM

T-STRAP METAL CONNECTOR

CUT ALONG THE LINE marking the shoulder of a notch across the top end of a post using a reciprocating saw with a long wood-cutting blade (above, left). Making both shoulder cuts will remove the waste area. Use a circular saw to make the shoulder cuts if you have difficulty keeping the reciprocating blade aligned with the marks. A reciprocating saw is necessary to complete the cuts. Cut a notch across the end of a post when it will hold a beam (above, right). This is an alternative to installing the beam on top of the post (see page 101). Some local codes require an additional metal framing connector. The bottom end of a railing post is notched so it will rest on top of the decking (see page 97). Notches across post ends also can be made using this method.

CUTTING AN INSIDE CORNER NOTCH

1 **BEGIN THE FIRST** long shoulder cut with a circular saw. Set the blade depth equal to the depth of the notch (see Step 5). Since this type of notch usually is cut in a 4x4, it may be helpful to place another 4×4 next to the one you cut to help support the saw, or clamp a straightedge guide to an extra 4x4 to guide the cut.

2 **STOP CUTTING** when the blade touches the line marking the end of the notch. Wait for the blade to quit spinning before removing it from the post.

3 **MAKE THE CUT** for the shoulder at the top of the notch after cutting the other long shoulder. Stop cutting when the blade touches the long shoulder cut.

Homer's Hindsight

MEASURE EACH POST

I had a dozen posts to notch before dinner and thought working on the posts one at a time would be quicker. I marked and cut the notch for one, then used it to mark the next post. I cut that one and used it to mark the next post and so on until all the posts were notched. I lined them up to admire my work and saw that the notch location was $1/4$ inch off between the first and last posts! Some of my cuts weren't accurate and using each newly cut post to mark the next only increased my mistakes. My appetite cost me big time!

4 **CUT THROUGH THE REMAINING WOOD** at the top of the notch using a sharp chisel to release the waste material from the notch. Use the chisel to clean out the corner and to make it square.

5 **AN INSIDE CORNER NOTCH** usually is cut in a 4×4 railing post that straddles a corner of the deck. This prevents the need to install posts on both sides of the deck corner for some railing styles.

CUTTING AN OUTSIDE CORNER NOTCH

1 **USE A CIRCULAR SAW** to make the long shoulder cuts (see page 96). Stop the saw blade inside the marks. Mark the notch layout so the beam and rim joist will rest in the notch cut on adjacent post faces (see Step 3).

2 **USE A RECIPROCATING SAW** with a wood cutting blade to complete the cuts, if necessary. Use a chisel to finish out the corners.

3 **AN OUTSIDE CORNER NOTCH** is made in a corner post where a beam and rim joist meet. The beam and joist pieces sit in the notch instead of being attached to the top of the post with metal framing connectors (see page 17). See inset above for a stronger outside corner notch option.

OPTION FOR A STRONGER OUTSIDE CORNER NOTCH

SECURE BOARDS IN NOTCHES

Attaching beams and rim joists to posts by securing them in notches is an alternative to using metal framing connectors. Many local codes allow this method. You may think the deck is more attractive without the metal and you'll save the cost of connectors. However, cutting notches is more difficult and takes more time than using connectors. Check local codes—some codes allow notching but require an additional metal connector. If that's the case, just use connectors.

BUILDING AND INSTALLING BEAMS

Most beams are made of pieces of 2× lumber fastened together. Solid lumber at least 4×6 in size that is long enough for beams is difficult to find in many parts of the country. A solid lumber beam also is more expensive than an equivalent beam built from 2× lumber. A 2×-lumber beam longer than 12 feet may be easier to build in place on the posts.

Pages 99–100 show how to build a beam from 2×10 lumber on the ground before raising it into position. The project on pages 101–103 shows long 2×12 beams installed piece by piece on top of the posts. Making a beam from pieces of 2×12 lumber that are sandwiched around posts is shown on pages 106–107. Although allowed by building code, this is the weakest beam type and additional metal connectors usually are required (see page 17).

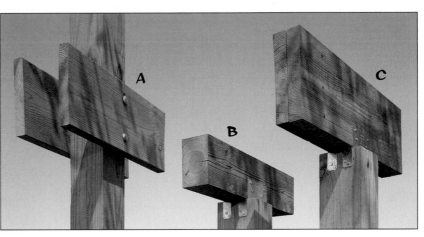

THE THREE BASIC BEAM TYPES: (A) Two pieces of 2× lumber sandwiched around posts. Although allowed by building code, this type of beam is not as strong as the others. (B) A solid, large piece of lumber (4×6 minimum) that is attached to post tops. (C) Two or more pieces of 2× lumber fastened together to form a beam that is attached to post tops.

SKILL SCALE

EASY	MEDIUM	HARD

SKILLS: Cutting lumber, driving fasteners, applying caulk.

HOW LONG WILL IT TAKE?

PROJECT: Building a 16-foot beam from 2×10 lumber on the ground.

EXPERIENCED . . . . 45 MIN.

HANDY . . . . 1.5 HR.

NOVICE . . . . 2 HR.

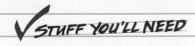

✓ **STUFF YOU'LL NEED**

TOOLS: Tape measure, circular saw, drill, hammer, caulk gun.

MATERIALS: Lumber, fasteners, post caps, caulk.

BUILDING BEAMS FROM 2X LUMBER

1 **ALIGN EDGES** of the boards that will form the beam and clamp them together. Place the crown sides (see page 14) facing the beam. Make a long beam from shorter pieces of lumber so that splices between pieces will be centered over posts (see Step 3). Stagger the splices on opposite sides of the beam. **Note: On a beam where joists will attach to its inside face, the boards on the inside face should be 1½ inch shorter at each end of the beam. This space is for the outside rim joist (see page 107).**

FRAMING

2 **ATTACH THE BOARDS** with 3-inch galvanized deck screws. Drive the screws at a slight angle. Space three screws at each end of the board every 2 feet down its length. Screws should be no closer than 1½ inches to the board edges.

3 **RAISE THE BEAM** and set it into post caps (see page 17) installed on the post tops, using a helper. Level the beam using cedar shims if necessary. Drive a nail through each hole in the cap flanges. Use nails specified by the post cap manufacturer.

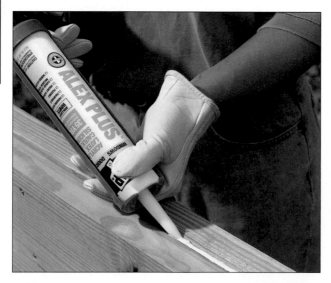

4 **OPTION A:** Caulk the seam between boards with acrylic latex caulk with silicone to prevent moisture penetration. This extra protection increases the durability of a beam made from pressure-treated lumber. Wear gloves when working with silicone caulk to protect your skin.

OPTION B: Apply self-sealing membrane (see page 16) over the top surface of a beam in wet climate zones. Cut a strip of membrane about 6 inches wide. Roll it with the protective paper backing facing out. Place the rolled membrane at one end of the beam, overlapping the beam evenly on both sides. Peel back about one foot of the paper backing and press the self-adhesive surface onto the beam. Continue peeling and applying the membrane as you unroll it. Overlap seams 3 inches between strips of membrane.

INSTALLING BEAMS ON TOP OF POSTS

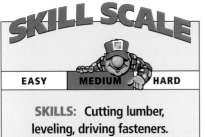

EASY   **MEDIUM**   **HARD**

SKILLS: Cutting lumber, leveling, driving fasteners.

HOW LONG WILL IT TAKE?

PROJECT: Building a beam on top of posts, with a helper and scaffolding in place.

EXPERIENCED . . . . . . 1 HR.

HANDY . . . . 1.25 HR.

NOVICE . . . . 1.5 HR.

✔ STUFF YOU'LL NEED

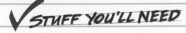

TOOLS: Tape measure, hammer, circular saw, level, drill.

MATERIALS: Lumber, post caps, angle brackets, fasteners, cedar shims.

1 **ATTACH POST CAPS** (see page 17) to the post tops. Use spacers cut from scrap 2× lumber when installing adjustable caps. Position the post caps so the beam will be the correct distance from the ledger board. The outside faces of the beam are usually flush with the outside faces of the posts; check your plan to be certain.

Scaffolding provides a safe, sturdy work surface.

2 **INSTALL THE FIRST ROW** of 2× lumber boards for the outside face of the beam. Position them against the outside flanges of the post caps. Center splices over posts. Ends of boards should butt together without gaps. Level the boards using cedar shims, if necessary. Drive one nail through a hole in each post cap to hold the boards in place.

3 **PLACE THE BOARDS** for the inner face of the beam between the first row of boards and the inside flanges of the post caps. Seams between boards for the inner face should be centered on different posts than the seams in the first row. Fasten the boards for the inner face to the 2× already installed. Note: The boards on the inner face of the beam in this project are 1½ inches shorter at each end of the beam (see Step 5).

FRAMING

4 **MEASURE BETWEEN THE BEAM** and house at each post to make sure the distance is equal. Adjust by repositioning the temporary braces. Make certain the beam face is vertical before measuring.

5 **FIT THE FIRST BOARD** for a perpendicular beam in the 1½-inch-wide space at one end of the first beam. Usually only a single rim joist (see page 109) is needed on a deck where joists attach to the inner beam face. Because this deck will become a four-season addition in the future, perpendicular beams are necessary to carry the extra weight of the addition. Perpendicular beams also are necessary for some other deck designs (see page 103).

6 **DRIVE 3-INCH GALVANIZED DECK SCREWS** through the overlapping piece of the first beam into the end of the board. Space screws 2 to 3 inches apart. If the beam face isn't vertical, temporarily hold the board with the end butting against the beam before driving the screws. Then place the board into the post caps. On this project, the perpendicular beam sits on an additional post and in a double joist hanger (see page 18) at the ledger.

7 **POSITION AND ATTACH BOARDS** for the inner face of the perpendicular beam, as in Step 3. The first board butts against the inner face of the first beam. Since the beam sits in a hanger at the ledger, the inner face of the beam is 1½ inches shorter than the outer face (see Step 9).

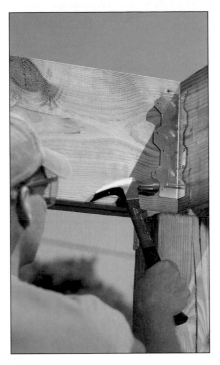

8 **ATTACH AN ANGLE BRACKET** (see page 18) to reinforce the corner between beams, using as large a bracket as the corner will allow. Use nails specified by the bracket manufacturer.

9 **INSTALL THE PERPENDICULAR BEAM** at the other end of the first beam following the basic method shown in Steps 5 through 8. The ends of the outer face fit in the 1½-inch-wide gaps at the end of the ledger (see page 102) and the first beam. The inner face of the perpendicular beam is 3 inches shorter than the outer face and butts against the ledger and the inner face of the first beam. Attach an angle bracket in both corners. Leave temporary bracing in place until you begin installing decking boards.

CLOSER LOOK

SUPPORT FROM BELOW

In some deck designs, a beam supports the joists from underneath rather than from joist hangers attached to its face (see page 18). This allows the joists to be cantilevered beyond the beam up to one-fourth the length of the span (see page 9). Check your local code about allowable cantilever distances. Build this type of beam from 2× lumber, as shown on page 100. The boards on both beam faces are the same length—don't make a 1½-inch gap at the ends of the inner face. If you install joists that are narrower than the ledger, level and trim posts so they position the beam to support the bottoms of the joists.

103

INSTALLING BEAMS AT 45 DEGREES

Install a beam at a 45-degree angle in the interior of a deck to support diagonal decking patterns or where a deck wraps around a corner. A perimeter beam installed at a 45-degree angle changes the shape of the deck.

WORK SMARTER

FILL THE GAP

There will be a ½-inch gap remaining when a beam made of two pieces of 2× lumber is placed in a nonadjustable post cap for 4×4 posts (see page 17). Fill this gap with a shim made from ½-inch pressure-treated plywood.

Cut the shim slightly larger than the post cap flange. Caulk the seams around the shim with silicone caulk. Place the shim on the side of the beam where it will be least visible.

1 **MARK THE POINT** where each side of the 45-degree beam intersects the existing framing at the corner. It is easier to mark and install a beam at 45 degrees after the right angle framing is installed. Cut the boards for the beam several inches longer than needed. Clamp the boards together and rest them on the existing framing to mark beam length accurately. Unclamp the boards, then cut them to length with a circular saw blade set at 45 degrees (see page 28).

2 **INSTALL ONE SIDE** of the beam first. Drive screws through the beam board into the existing framing. Drill pilot holes (see page 23) before driving screws to prevent splitting the end of the board; then attach the other side of the beam (see page 101).

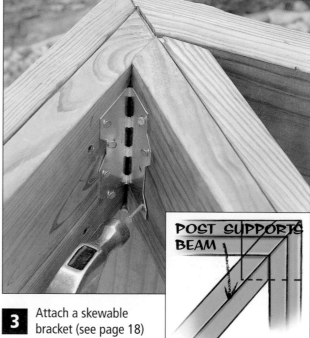

POST SUPPORTS BEAM

3 Attach a skewable bracket (see page 18) to reinforce the corner on each side of the beam. Use as large a bracket as the corner will allow.

FRAMING

45-DEGREE PERIMETER BEAM

Some deck designs require that a beam be installed at 45 degrees on the perimeter of the deck. The framing that the 45-degree beam attaches to should be installed first. Cut boards for the 45-degree beam longer than needed. Clamp them together and mark the length, as shown on page 104. Cut the ends of the 45-degree beam and the framing to which it attaches at 22½-degree angles (see page 118).

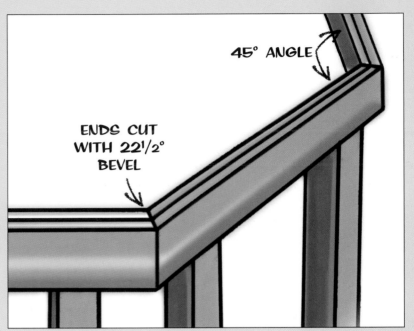

45° ANGLE

ENDS CUT WITH 22½° BEVEL

INSTALLING BEAMS ON FOOTINGS

Make sure you've given the concrete time to cure.

1 **ATTACH A BEAM** to post anchors (see page 18) installed on footings. Each end of a beam should be within 1 foot of a footing. Build the beam as shown on pages 99–100. The inside faces should be 1½ inches shorter than the outer face at each end of the beams. Rim joists will be installed in this gap (see pages 102 and 109).

2 **MEASURE THE DIAGONALS** between beam ends. Adjust post anchor positions until the measurements are equal to square the deck structure. Install joists as shown on pages 109–111.

SANDWICHING A BEAM AROUND POSTS

SKILL SCALE

EASY   **MEDIUM**   HARD

SKILLS: Cutting and drilling lumber, driving fasteners.

HOW LONG WILL IT TAKE?

PROJECT: Sandwiching a beam around posts, with a helper and scaffolding in place.

EXPERIENCED . . . . . . 1 HR.

HANDY . . . . 1.25 HR.

NOVICE . . . . 1.5 HR.

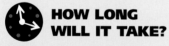

✓ STUFF YOU'LL NEED

TOOLS: Tape measure, level, chalk line, circular saw, drill, ratchet and socket.

MATERIALS: Lumber, fasteners.

1 **SNAP A CHALK LINE** to mark the top of the beam location across the posts. Use a water level to accurately mark the correct beam height (see page 24). Make certain the line across the posts is level. Note: An option for building a sandwiched beam is to attach the boards in notches cut in the posts (see page 95). If you choose this method, cut the notches at this time.

2 **ATTACH THE FIRST BOARD** for the beam on the inner face of the posts. Drive two screws at each post to hold it in position. The ends of the inner beam should be flush with post edges. Place a splice between boards at the center of a post if you need more than one board for a long beam. Attach the outer beam board similarly. Make the outer beam board 1½ inches longer than the inner beam board at each end if a rim joist will be installed (see page 109).

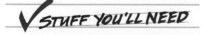

3 **DRILL HOLES** for two ½-inch-diameter carriage bolts at each post through both beam boards and the post. Center each hole about 2 inches from an edge. Stagger the holes on either side of the center of the post to prevent splitting. Attach metal connectors if required by local code (see page 17).

4 **TIGHTEN A NUT** over the end of each carriage bolt with a ratchet and socket. Place a washer over the bolt before installing the nut. Tighten each nut until the washer begins to sink into the wood. Check the nuts after 24 hours and retighten as necessary.

5 **INSTALL THE RIM JOIST** or perpendicular beam, depending on the deck design. Some codes require installation of an additional metal framing connector on this type of beam (see page 18). Trim the post top flush with the top of the beam (see page 94).

POST BRACING

Local code may require permanent bracing of deck posts. This is most common on attached decks over 8 feet high and freestanding decks over 3 feet high. The size and number of posts also affect this requirement. Posts supporting a small raised stair landing often require permanent bracing (see page 145). This type of bracing also will be determined by local code. Attach bracing before installing joists.

1 **ATTACH PERMANENT BRACING** with lag screws or carriage bolts (see page 16). Make bracing from 4- to 6-inch-wide pressure-treated lumber. Use 6-inch-wide lumber for braces over 8 feet long. Install bracing at a 45-degree angle to posts.

2 **CUT BRACE PIECES** to length so the cut ends are vertical when installed. Leave a 1/8- to 1/4-inch gap between pieces that meet on a post to prevent trapping moisture. Use deck screws to position bracing before drilling holes and driving permanent fasteners.

3 **ATTACH A SHORT PIECE** of post between X-bracing (see below) for stability. The piece should be at least 9 inches long to prevent splitting. Fasten it with lag screws or a carriage bolt.

CLOSER LOOK

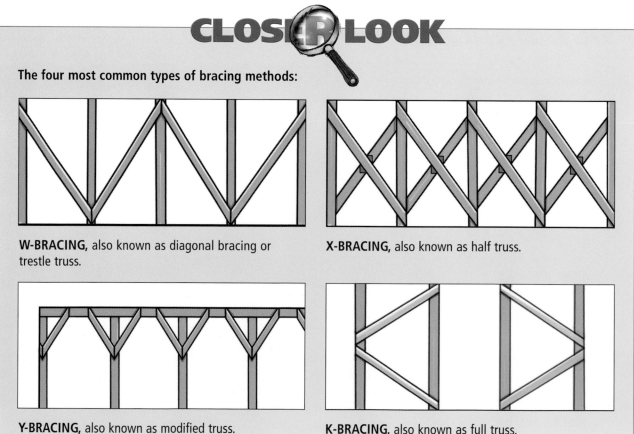

The four most common types of bracing methods:

W-BRACING, also known as diagonal bracing or trestle truss.

X-BRACING, also known as half truss.

Y-BRACING, also known as modified truss.

K-BRACING, also known as full truss.

INSTALLING JOISTS

Joists support the decking. Install them with 12-, 16-, or 24-inch spacing between their centers, depending on the thickness of decking material, the installation pattern of the decking, and local building codes (page 9). Choose quality lumber that is as straight as possible and make certain each joist is installed with its crown side facing up (see page 14). Attach joists to framing with metal joist hangers for the strongest connections. The joists on this project are 15 feet long, installed 16 inches on center, and sit on top of the beam. They are cantilevered (see pages 6, 9) about 2 feet beyond the beam.

DOUBLE JOIST HANGER

SINGLE JOIST HANGER

45° JOIST HANGER

SKILL SCALE

EASY **MEDIUM** HARD

SKILLS: Measuring and cutting lumber, driving fasteners.

HOW LONG WILL IT TAKE?

PROJECT: Installing joists for a 16×12-foot deck, assuming you can stand on the ground rather than on scaffolding.

EXPERIENCED . . . . 30 MIN.

HANDY . . . . 45 MIN.

NOVICE . . . . 1 HR.

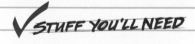

✓ STUFF YOU'LL NEED

TOOLS: Tape measure, speed square, circular saw, drill, hammer.

MATERIALS: Lumber, fasteners, seismic ties, angle brackets.

1 **MARK A BOARD** of the correct dimension for one rim joist (see page 4). Check your design plan for the distance that the outer edge of the deck should be from the ledger. The length of the rim joist should be equal to this distance. Make certain the other end of the board is square before measuring and making this mark.

2 **CUT THE BOARD** to length using a large speed square to guide a straight cut (see page 26).

3 **ATTACH ONE END** of the rim joist to the end of the ledger with 3-inch deck screws. Rest the opposite end on the beam. The board should fit against the house sheathing in the 1½-inch-wide gap between the end of the ledger and the siding (see page 44). Note: Local code may require a rim joist made from doubled 2× lumber.

4 **DRIVE A SCREW** to temporarily "toenail" the rim joist to the beam. The outer face of the joist should be flush with the end of the beam.

5 **ATTACH THE RIM JOIST** at the other end of the beam. The deck in this project fits in a corner of the house. The rim joist is fastened to the house framing as well as to the end of the beam. Flashing is installed over the rim joist just as it was on the ledger (see page 46). Note the gap in the house siding at the end of the rim joist, providing space for the header joist (see page 4).

6 **FASTEN THE HEADER JOIST** (see page 4) to the ends of the rim joists after cutting it to length. Space 3-inch deck screws 2 to 3 inches apart. Drill pilot holes to prevent splitting the end of the board.

7 **MEASURE THE DIAGONALS** of the rectangle made by the ledger, rim joists, and header joist. Adjust the positions until the measurements are equal. Back out the screws, toenailing the rim joists to adjust the positions if necessary.

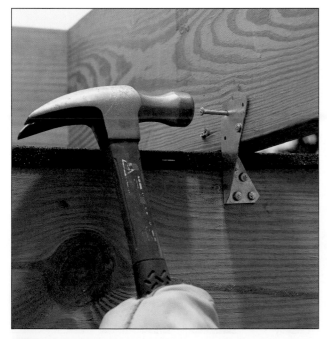

8 **FASTEN THE RIM JOISTS** permanently to the beam with metal framing connectors called seismic ties (see page 17). Use nails specified by the connector manufacturer.

9 **ATTACH AN ANGLE BRACKET** in each corner of the joist frame to reinforce the joint. Use as long a bracket as the lumber size allows. Stacking two shorter brackets is acceptable.

Measure at each joist location to determine the cutting length for the joist. An option is to install rough-cut joists several inches longer than necessary and trim them to length in place (see page 117). If you choose this option, install the header joist after the joists are trimmed to length.

SKILL SCALE

EASY **MEDIUM** HARD

SKILLS: Measuring and cutting lumber, driving fasteners.

HOW LONG WILL IT TAKE?

PROJECT: Installing interior joists on a 12×16-foot deck.

EXPERIENCED . . . . 2.5 HR.

HANDY . . . . 4 HR.

NOVICE . . . . 6 HR.

✔ STUFF YOU'LL NEED

TOOLS: Tape measure, speed square, circular saw, drill, hammer.

MATERIALS: Lumber, fasteners, joist hangers.

1 **MARK ONE EDGE** for each joist location on the inner face of the header joist. Mark the same edge for each location. Start measuring and marking the header joist from the same end you started measuring the ledger on so the marks align (page 45). Use a speed square to mark vertical lines.

2 **MEASURE AND MARK** the 1½-inch-board thickness at each joist location. Mark the other vertical line for each joist location using a speed square.

3 **ATTACH ONE SIDE** of a joist hanger (see page 18) at the center joist location on the header joist and the ledger, using nails specified by the hanger manufacturer. Measure the exact height of the board you will use for this joist before attaching the hangers. Position the top surface of the bottom flange on each hanger at this distance from the top edge of header joist and ledger to align the top edge of the joist with the top edges of header joist and ledger. Note: The option is to install joists first, driving fasteners through the header joist into the joist ends. Then attach the joist hangers.

4 **PLACE THE JOIST** into the open joist hangers after cutting it to length. Double-check its length before setting it in place. It is important that this joist match the measurement in Step 13. Make certain the crown edge faces up.

Homer's Hindsight

NOT ALL JOISTS ARE EQUAL
I thought it would be a lot more efficient to attach all the joist hangers at one time. I measured the width of one 2×10 joist and set the hangers at this distance. After installing the joists, I noticed that many of the top edges were either higher or lower than the header joist and ledger. I measured each joist and found over 1/4-inch difference in width between the narrowest and widest boards! I didn't feel so efficient after struggling for several hours to fix this mess.

5 **FASTEN THE OTHER HANGER** side around the joist at the ledger. Attach the hanger to the ledger first. Then drive nails through the hanger into the joist on both sides of the hanger. Butt the end of the joist against the ledger. Drive a nail through every nail hole in the hanger—the strength of the hanger connection depends on this step.

6 **OPTION A:** Attach the hanger around the joist at the header joist in a similar manner. Have your helper push against the header joist to make a tight joint between the boards before driving nails through the hanger into the end of the joist.

6 **OPTION B:** Use a clamp to draw the header joist tight against the end of the joist if you're working alone. Drive a nail or screw into the joist near its end. Leave about ¾ inch of the fastener visible to provide a clamping point on the joist.

7 **INSTALL THE REMAINING JOISTS.** Measure for joist length at each location for best results. Attach each joist hanger based on the actual height of the board it will hold.

DOUBLE-DUTY JOIST HANGERS

A double joist hanger (see page 18) fastens the ends of two joists (or a beam) to the vertical face of another framing member. Double joists are necessary for several decking patterns (see page 10). Locate and attach one side of two double joist hangers just as you would regular joist hangers, but place both joists into the hangers before closing and nailing the other sides (above, left). Fasten the joists together with 3-inch deck screws as when making a beam (see page 100). Use clamps to force joist faces together and to align edges, if necessary (above, right). Begin joist alignment over the beam on decks where joists attach to the top of the beam.

FRAMING

INSTALLING BLOCKING

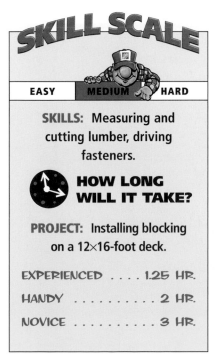

SKILL SCALE

| EASY | MEDIUM | HARD |

SKILLS: Measuring and cutting lumber, driving fasteners.

HOW LONG WILL IT TAKE?

PROJECT: Installing blocking on a 12×16-foot deck.

EXPERIENCED . . . . 1.25 HR.

HANDY . . . . 2 HR.

NOVICE . . . . 3 HR.

Install blocking between joists to prevent twisting of the joists on spans longer than 8 feet. Measure, cut, and install blocking pieces carefully to prevent bowing of the joists.

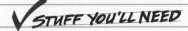

STUFF YOU'LL NEED

TOOLS: Tape measure, chalk line, speed square, circular saw, hammer.

MATERIALS: Lumber, fasteners.

1 **SNAP A CHALK LINE** across joists at the center of a joist span. This line locates the position for blocking pieces.

Alternate blocking to make nailing easy.

2 **NAIL BLOCKING PIECES** between the joists with 3-inch galvanized spiral shank nails. Attach blocking between adjacent joists on opposite sides of the line to allow you to drive nails into board ends rather than toe-nailing. Make blocking from the same dimension lumber as the joists. Measure the distance between two joists at the ledger or header joist to determine the length for the blocking between them.

3 **ATTACH A METAL FRAMING CONNECTOR,** called a rafter tie (see page 17), to fasten each joist to the beam. This is a stronger connection than toenailing the joist to the beam. Drive a nail through every nail hole in the connector using nails specified by the manufacturer. Install ties on the less visible side of the beam, if possible.

CLOSER LOOK

TWO WAYS TO SPLICE JOISTS

Many deck designs require joists longer than are available in dimension lumber. Make a long joist by splicing two shorter pieces of 2× lumber together. The splice must be centered over a beam. One splicing method is to butt the ends of two boards over a beam (below, left). Make certain there is a tight fit between the boards. A nailing plate (see page 18) reinforces the joint and rafter ties attach the boards to the beam. The other method overlaps the board ends over a beam (below, right). Boards should overlap 12 inches and are fastened together with 3-inch deck screws. A seismic tie attaches each board to the beam. The butt joint method uses less wood and keeps the decking screws in a straight line. An overlap splice is quicker to make but creates an offset line of screws in the decking that you may find less attractive.

NAILING PLATE

RAFTER OR "HURRICANE" TIE

SEISMIC TIES

TRIMMING JOISTS TO LENGTH IN PLACE

1 **SNAP A CHALK LINE** across joists at the length required for the deck. First install the joists in joist hangers at the ledger as shown on page 109–111. Boards should be longer than the required final length. Temporarily attach the joists to the top of the beam with toenailing screws (see page 16). Outer faces of the rim joists should be flush with the ends of the beam. Spacing between joists is identical to spacing at the ledger. Tack a 1×4 brace across the tops of the joists for stability.

2 **MARK A VERTICAL CUTTING LINE** on the face of each joist at the chalk line. Measure and mark another line on the ledger side of the first line. The distance between the lines should be equal to the distance between the saw blade and the edge of the base plate on a circular saw. Attach a temporary cutting guide made from 1×4 stock at this line.

3 **TRIM EACH JOIST** to length with a circular saw. Keep the edge of the base plate firmly against the temporary cutting guide throughout each cut so the joist ends are square. An option for tall decks is to attach decking across the joists close enough to the joist ends so the joists can be trimmed to length from above. This is safer than working on a tall ladder. Safety Note: Make certain you have stable footing or a secure ladder before cutting each joist. A circular saw is heavy and can kick back during cutting.

4 **ATTACH JOIST HANGERS** around the joists to permanently connect them to the header joist. First cut the header joist to length and fasten it to the joist ends with nails. Measure the diagonals (see page 105) and make adjustments until they're equal. Remove the temporary toenailing screws, if necessary, to adjust joist positions. Install blocking if needed (see page 116). Permanently attach joists to the beam with rafter ties after installing joist hangers and blocking.

FRAMING

INSTALLING JOISTS AT 45-DEGREE ANGLES

Installing joists at 45-degree angles is relatively easy with 45-degree joist hangers (see page 18). Joists must be installed at 45-degree angles when making a 45-degree-angled corner on a deck, as in this project. Two board ends cut at $22\frac{1}{2}$-degree angles meet to form the correct 45-degree angle. Use a speed square to establish the angles. Joists in this deck project attach to the top of the beam. Local code may require doubled rim joists. See page 105

for information about making a 45-degree corner on a deck with perimeter beams. Measure three or four times before cutting boards at angles.

1 **ATTACH THE HEADER JOIST** temporarily to the ends of the joists using screws. Cut the header joist long enough to extend past the point where it will intersect the 45-degree corner. Install the joists as shown on pages 112–114. The rim joist also extends past the corner intersection. Note that the beam extends past the 45-degree corner (see Step 6). Attach temporary braces across the joist tops for stability.

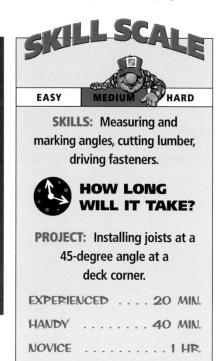

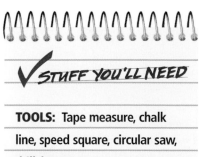

2 **SNAP A CHALK LINE** across the header joist, rim joist, and interior joists to mark the 45-degree corner at the location indicated by your deck plan (see page 11).

FRAMING

118

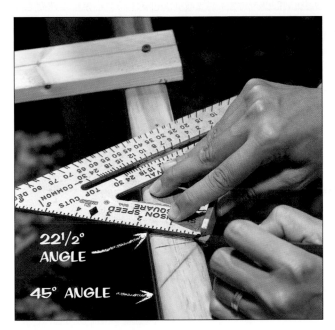

3 **CHANGE THE 45-DEGREE ANGLE** marked by the chalk line on the rim joist to a 22½-degree angle. Mark the 22½-degree angle from the point where the chalk line touches the outer face of the rim joist. The 22½-angle faces away from the 45-degree angle. Repeat for the 45-degree angle marked by the chalk line on the header joist. Test the angles on scrap pieces before cutting joists.

4 **CUT THE END** of the rim joist and the header joist with the blade setting at 22½ degrees. Then cut the joist ends with a circular saw blade at a 45-degree angle. Use a temporary cutting guide to make each cut (see page 117). Safety Note: Make certain you have stable footing or a secure ladder before cutting.

5 **MARK A CUTTING LINE** at each end of the board that will be the header joist for the 45-degree corner. Place a board that is slightly longer than needed on top of the rim joist and header joist. Align its outer face with the corners of the cut ends on the header joist and rim joist. Mark a vertical line at this intersection on each end. Cut the board to length with the circular saw blade setting at 22½ degrees. The outer face of the board should be longer than the inner face.

6 **DRIVE 3-INCH DECK SCREWS** through the header joist and rim joist into the 45-degree corner header joist. Space the screws 2 to 3 inches apart. Angle the screws into the center of the 45-degree corner header joist, drilling pilot holes to prevent splitting. Reinforce the 45-degree corners with skewable brackets (see page 18). Attach joist ends to the 45-degree corner header joist with 45-degree joist hangers (see page 18). Cut the end of the beam with a reciprocating saw so it is flush with the outer face of the 45-degree corner header joist.

WORK SMARTER

HANGING 45s

A 45-degree joist hanger makes a strong connection when attaching a joist at a 45-degree angle. The hanger is forgiving—even if the joist and framing don't fit together tightly, the depth of the hanger allows for a secure connection. Mark a 2⅛-inch-wide joist location. That is the distance across the face of a 45-degree angled cut in 2× lumber. Attach one side of the hanger to the header joist or beam (above, left) as you would a regular joist hanger (see page 18). Cut the end of the joist at a 45-degree angle and place it in the hanger. Close the other side of the hanger and drive nails through every nail hole in the hanger (above, right). Both left- and right-facing 45-degree joist hangers are available (above, left).

INSTALLING JOISTS AROUND OBSTRUCTIONS

SKILL SCALE

EASY **MEDIUM** HARD

SKILLS: Measuring and cutting lumber, driving fasteners.

HOW LONG WILL IT TAKE?

PROJECT: Installing joists around a mature tree.

EXPERIENCED . . . . 20 MIN.

HANDY . . . . 40 MIN.

NOVICE . . . . 1 HR.

Framing around obstructions such as trees, rocks, or spas usually requires that at least one joist position be interrupted. The obstruction requires double joists around the obstacle in order to support the ends of the interrupted joists. Check with local code if your installation requires interrupting more than two joists; additional posts and beams may be necessary. Frame openings around trees to allow room for future growth. The diameter of the mature poplar trunk shown in this project will not increase significantly.

STUFF YOU'LL NEED

TOOLS: Tape measure, speed square, circular saw, hammer.

MATERIALS: Lumber, fasteners, joist hangers.

1 **INSTALL DOUBLE JOISTS** in double joist hangers on both sides of the obstruction. Attach the other joists between beams or other framing members as shown on pages 109–111. Place rock or mulch before framing.

2 **ATTACH SHORT DOUBLE JOISTS** between the long double joists to complete the framing around the obstruction. The short double joists also should be installed with double joist hangers.

3 **INSTALL THE REMAINING JOIST PIECES** between the beams and the short double joists. The short double joists allow installation of joists at the correct spacing necessary for adequate decking support.

4 **CUT AND ATTACH DECKING** to the joists as shown on pages 124–132. Note: This is a mature tree and the diameter of the trunk will not increase significantly. Allow more space around immature trees.

FRAMING

6 DECKING

Decking is the most visible part of the deck. It can be fastened across joists in an attractive pattern (see page 10), stiffening and strengthening the deck structure. Choose good-looking boards and install them neatly for the best appearance. Use a sharp blade in a miter saw or circular saw when cutting decking to get crisp edges without splintering. Leave temporary bracing in place until at least the first few decking boards are installed.

Choose a railing style for your deck before installing decking. Some styles require posts to be installed before decking is installed.

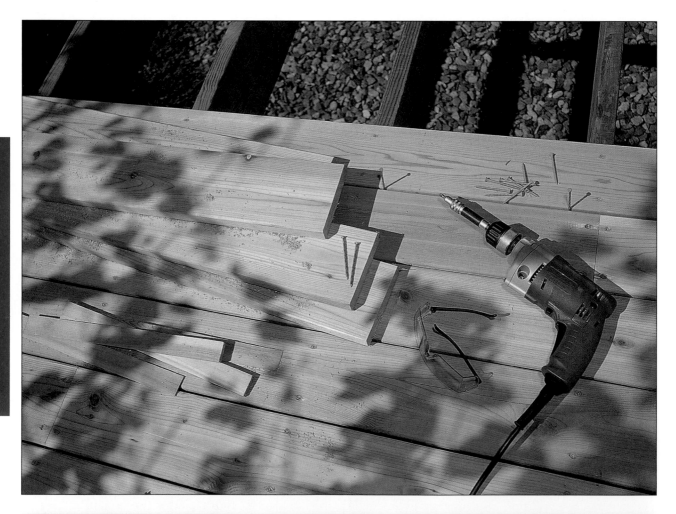

DECKING FASTENERS

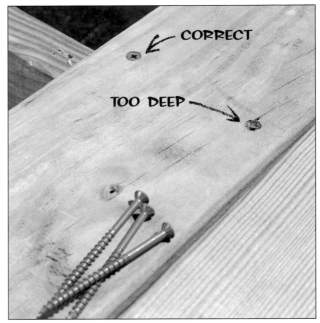

DECK SCREWS OR SPIRAL SHANK NAILS are the most common decking fasteners. Use only fasteners that are galvanized, stainless steel, or have rustproof coatings. Deck screws are available with colored coatings that blend with the wood color of the decking used. Make certain you have a screw tip that matches the head of the screws you use. See pages 133–135 for systems that attach decking invisibly.

DRIVE EACH DECK SCREW so the head surface is flush with the surface of the board. A screw driven too deeply creates an unattractive hole that collects moisture and debris. Use screws long enough to penetrate into the joists as deep as the thickness of the decking. For example, use 2½-inch screws to attach 5/4×6 decking.

HAMMER A SPIRAL SHANK NAIL at an angle through the decking into the joist. Angle a pair of nails toward each other at each joist to give the nails better holding power.

USE A NAIL SET to drive each nailhead surface flush with the surface of the board. A hammer will create a dimple in the board surface if you try to do this without the nail set.

INSTALLING DECKING

Decking is usually 2x4, 2x6, or ⁵/4x6 boards installed on wide faces. There are several common installation patterns (see page 10). Extra blocking must be installed for some patterns so both ends of each board are supported. The more complicated the decking pattern, the more important it is to do a dry run before you cut boards to lay out the angles and joints. Arrange boards with the fewest possible end-to-end seams, and stagger the seams for the best appearance. For a small deck, buy lumber long enough to span the entire width of the deck.

Find boards that are as straight as possible. Installation can straighten a small amount of twisting or bowing. Return boards that are more than a little crooked. Buy about 10 percent more decking than you estimate is necessary to allow for returns and for cutting waste during installation. For diagonal patterns buy about 15 percent more.

Growth rings visible in the end grain of a decking board indicate which side of the board was closest to the bark side of the tree from which it came. Professional carpenters disagree whether the bark side should face up or down during installation. The best solution is to properly fasten each board so its best-looking side is visible. Deck screws make the strongest connection but have larger, more visible heads than nails (see page 123). Look for color screws that match decking. The cedar decking for the upper level on this project was installed perpendicular to the joists and fastened with deck screws.

SKILL SCALE

EASY   MEDIUM   HARD

SKILLS: Measuring and cutting lumber, driving fasteners.

🕐 HOW LONG WILL IT TAKE?

PROJECT: Installing decking on a 16×12-foot deck.

EXPERIENCED . . . . . 3 HR.

HANDY . . . . 4 HR.

NOVICE . . . . 5 HR.

✓ STUFF YOU'LL NEED

TOOLS: Tape measure, chalk line, power miter saw, jig saw, drill, pry bar, speed square.

MATERIALS: Lumber, fasteners.

1 **MEASURE BETWEEN THE OUTSIDE** of the header joist and the house at the top of the ledger. Do this at the center and corners of the deck to determine whether the distances are equal. Mark each rim joist at a distance from the outside of the header joist equal to the width of one decking board. (If your deck will have fascia boards, mark this distance from the outside face of the fascia attached to the header joist.) Make these marks at equal distances from the house. Note: Decking installation also can begin at the house with the final board attached at the header joist.

CLOSER LOOK

SPACING DECKING BOARDS

Gaps between decking boards allow water to drain off. Make consistently even gaps about 1/8 inch wide with spacers. Use either 8d or 10d nails and tap one into each joist so it rests against the installed board. Butt the next board tightly against the nails

before attaching; then remove the spacer nails. You may find it easier to use a spacer strip made from a straight piece of wood about 4 feet long (far left). Snap a chalk line down the center of the strip. Drive a nail every 16 inches through the chalk line so about 1 inch of the nail protrudes on the other side of the strip. Position the spacer so the ends of the nails are between boards. Another easy-to-use spacer is a long metal straightedge (near left) that usually is about 1/8 inch thick. Set the edge of the straightedge against the joists between boards. Ask at the lumberyard about the moisture content of the decking boards you buy before installing them with a gap. Wet wood will shrink when it dries. Butt the edges of wet boards against each other. The gap will appear as the wood shrinks.

2 **OPTION A:** Snap a chalk line across the marks on the rim joists. Check to make sure this line is parallel to the house. Begin decking installation with boards parallel to the house.

OPTION B: Adjust the chalk line position so it is closer to the header joist if the measurements in Step 1 aren't equal. Position the line so the widest distance between it and the outside edge of the header joist (or fascia board) is equal to the width of a decking board. The decking board will project beyond the header joist at the narrow distance. The board can be notched later if necessary (see page 129). Make certain the line is parallel to the house.

BUYER'S GUIDE

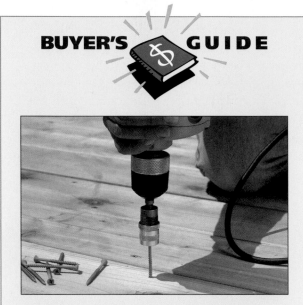

Buy an inexpensive screw depth-setting drill attachment so screw heads can be set flush with the decking surface easily and consistently. Use it with either cordless or corded drills. If you buy a drill, choose one with variable speed control and an adjustable clutch setting that will help prevent snapping screws.

3 **ALIGN THE FIRST ROW** of decking with the chalk line and attach the boards to the joists. The board end at the deck edge should protrude past the rim joist. Trim boards to length after installation (see page 117). Drive two fasteners through the board into the center of each joist. Position each fastener ³/₄ to 1 inch from the edge of the board.

4 **INSTALL THE NEXT ROW** of boards. Position spacers (see page 125) for a ¹/₈-inch gap. Butt each board against the spacers before fastening. If you have to use more than one board per row, center the ends over the joists.

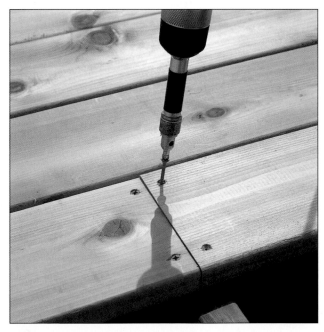

5 **DRIVE FASTENERS** through predrilled holes at the ends of boards. Predrilling prevents splitting of the wood by either screws or nails. Angle each fastener toward the center of the joist.

6 **MEASURE BETWEEN THE BACK** edge of the third row of decking and the house at several spots. Boards may vary in width so the distances may not be equal (they frequently aren't).

7 Snap another chalk line parallel to the house. Locate it at a distance from the third row that is equal to the width of a board plus the 1/8-inch gap. If the measurements in Step 6 aren't equal, position the line for the most uniform gap possible along the length of the row. Make sure the line is parallel to the house. Continue installing rows of decking. Measure and snap a new chalk line every third row to keep the decking parallel to the house.

8 Use a pry bar to pull a board toward the spacers, if necessary. Stick the points of the long end of the pry bar into the joist with the bar against the edge of the board. Pull on the pry bar to force the board against the spacers.

FORCING BOARDS INTO PLACE

Drive fasteners part way in a board before you "persuade" it into position. Align the fasteners over the joist and drive them until the points are almost through the board. Force the board against the spacer and finish driving the fasteners. This is much easier than trying to start a fastener into a board while pulling on a pry bar.

INSTALLING DECKING (CONTINUED)

9 **PUSH A WOOD SHIM** between boards (above, left) to create a gap, or use a pry bar to force boards apart (above, right). Protect the board you pry against with a wide putty knife to prevent damaging the board surface.

10 **INSTALL A SLIGHTLY BOWED BOARD** with the crown edge against the previously installed board. First position one end of the new board against the spacers.

11 **DRIVE TWO FASTENERS** at the end of the board. Make certain the board is tightly against the spacers before driving the fasteners.

12 **INSTALL FASTENERS** at the last joist where the board is firmly against the spacer.

HELPFUL METAL HANDS

A pry bar and long clamp, such as a pipe clamp, make it easy to force a bowed board into place. Insert the end of the short arm of the pry bar into a gap between two previously installed boards. Position one arm of the clamp against the pry bar and the other arm against the far edge of the bowed board. Operate the clamp to force the board against the spacers before driving fasteners.

13 **FORCE THE FAR END** of the board into position and attach it to the joist. Then drive fasteners at the remaining joist positions. Or you can work down the length of the board, forcing it into position and driving screws at each joist.

4 **MARK NOTCHES AROUND OBSTACLES** such as railing posts or legs for built-in benches. Position a board against the obstacle, aligning the board ends properly. Use a speed square to mark square lines.

15 **CUT THE NOTCH** with a jigsaw. Make the cuts on the outside of the marked lines to provide room for a good fit around the obstacle. Cut from both directions into the notch corners to make square corners.

DECKING

129

16 **INSTALL A NAILING CLEAT** to support the notched board where necessary. Make the cleat from a pressure-treated 2×4.

17 **TEST-FIT THE NOTCHED BOARD,** then attach the board with fasteners driven into joists and nailing cleats. Align the board properly along its entire length. Adjust the notch, if necessary, by trimming small amounts of material with a jigsaw or chisel.

18 **ATTACH THE LAST ROW** of decking at the house. Leave a ⅛-inch gap between the boards and the siding to prevent trapping moisture. Measure and cut the boards to a length that makes the ends flush with the rim joist (or fascia). The last row can't be cut in place because the wall prevents a saw from completing the cut. Cut the boards in the last row to width if necessary. A narrow row of decking is less noticeable against the house.

GUIDE TO MITER CUTS

Use a speed square as a quick guide for a 45-degree miter cut at the end of a decking board. It is easier to make an even 45-degree angled cut with a guide. This method also is handy if you use a power miter saw for most angled cuts. You may need to trim a board when it's not convenient to take the board to the power miter saw location.

DECKING

19 **OPTION A:** Tack a long, straight 1×4 temporarily onto the decking as a guide for a circular saw. Position the guide so the saw blade will trim boards at the proper length (see page 117). Use this technique if you're not sure you can make a long straight cut by following the chalk line. The temporary fasteners will leave a few small holes in the decking surface.

OPTION B: Trim decking to length with a circular saw. Snap a chalk line as a guide for the saw. Use the end of the last row (that was cut to length before installing) and the corner of the deck at the header joist as reference points for the chalk line. Set the saw to the proper depth so it just goes through the boards.

INSTALLING DECKING AT A 45-DEGREE ANGLE

EQUAL DISTANCE

SNAP A DIAGONAL CHALK LINE near the center of the deck area (above, left). Measure and mark equal distances from the 90-degree deck corner to establish a diagonal line at 45 degrees. Install the first board aligned with the line. Follow the basic decking installation methods shown on the previous pages. Snap a new chalk line after every three rows of decking (above, right). Measure from the edge of the board aligned with the first diagonal chalk line to keep the decking at a consistent angle. Install boards on one half of the deck, then return to the first diagonal line and install remaining decking. Let the boards hang over framing, and trim to the proper length after installation whenever possible; that's easier and quicker than measuring and cutting 45-degree miters on the ends of each board.

131

TRIMMING DECKING PATTERNS

DOUBLE JOIST

MANY DECKING PATTERNS have boards ending along a common line within the deck area (see page 10). Install decking as easily as possible by trimming boards to length along the line after installation wherever you can. For example, the decking on the project shown (above, left) will be installed diagonally from opposite directions and meet at a 45-degree angle in the center of the deck. Double joists at the deck center support the 45-degree mitered ends where they meet. Snap chalk lines and install decking on one side of the pattern as shown on page 131. Allow the boards to hang past the double joists. Snap a line across the boards and cut them over the seam between the joists (above, right). Adjust the saw-blade depth to cut through the decking but not into the joists.

CLOSER LOOK

ACCESS HATCH BLENDS INTO DECK SURFACE

Build an access hatch for a hose bib or other item beneath the decking surface. Attach 12-inch long cleats cut from pressure-treated 2×4s to the joists on both sides of the item (near right). The top of the cleats should be 3½ inches below the tops of the joists. Build a box frame from pressure-treated 2×4s. The frame length is equal to the distance between the joists minus ¼ inch. The frame width is equal to the width of the two decking boards in the last two rows next to the house. Remember to include the ⅛-inch gap between them. Use screws to fasten the frame pieces together. Cover the frame with pieces of decking cut to size (below, right). Drill two 1-inch-diameter holes in the decking to insert and remove the hatch.

DECKING

ALTERNATE DECKING FASTENING SYSTEMS

everal systems fasten decking to joists invisibly. The two basic types are clip systems and track systems. Clip systems (pages 133–135) typically fasten decking with small metal clips installed between board edges. Track systems (page 135) fasten the undersides of boards to metal track pieces installed on the joists.

Fastening decking with either of these systems takes significantly more time than using the traditional method. The additional hardware also increases the cost of the deck, but using one of these systems results in a deck surface with no visible fasteners.

Check the instructions for an alternate system before purchasing decking. Some decking systems require 2× lumber. Make certain decking lumber is dry when using a clip system. Wet lumber will shrink and that can affect the durability of the installation. Use the same basic methods for aligning boards parallel to the house as shown on pages 124–131.

DECKING CLIPS

1 **TOENAIL THE FIRST ROW** of decking boards at the header joist for a clip system. Drive 10-penny galvanized spiral shank nails (or deck screws) through both edges of the board at every joist location. Drill pilot holes for the fasteners to prevent splitting the board edge.

2 **ATTACH CLIPS** to one edge of each board for the next row of decking. First place each board in position and mark joist locations. Position a clip within 2 inches of every joist location. Attach clips with fasteners recommended by the clip manufacturer.

DECKING

133

DECKING CLIPS (CONTINUED)

3 **HOLD EACH BOARD** at a slight angle, and slide the clips under the edge of the first row of decking. Push boards as far forward as possible before placing them flat on the joists.

4 **USE A HAMMER** and a scrap wood block to seat each board firmly against the first row. The clips automatically create the proper gap between boards.

5 **TOENAIL THROUGH THE BACK EDGE** of the second row of boards. Drill pilot holes before driving fasteners. Make certain each board clip is firmly against the adjacent board before fastening. Use the same methods shown on page 128 to force a bowed board into position. Continue installing rows of decking.

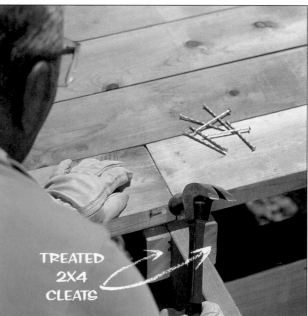

TREATED 2X4 CLEATS

6 **ADD CLEATS TO FASTEN A BOARD END** if you have an end seam between boards in a row of decking. Position the clip for the board in the next row within 2 inches of one of the cleats so the cleats won't obstruct the clip.

DECKING

USE LESS LUMBER

Save money on costly decking when installing boards on a multilevel deck. Plan to install decking on a lower level just up to box steps (below) or just beneath stringers on regular stairs.

7 **DRIVE NAILS** through the face of the boards in the last row of decking. There is no room for toenailing. Install clips and position the boards as in the other rows. Use a pry bar to force each board firmly against the previous row if necessary. Protect siding with a piece of scrap wood between the pry bar and siding. Use a nail set to drive nailheads beneath the surface of the boards. Fill the holes with exterior wood putty or colored caulk.

TRACK SYSTEM

SHORT PIECES OF METAL TRACK are attached to the joists with fasteners supplied by the manufacturer (above, left). Position them according to manufacturer's instructions. A common method has pieces attached on alternate sides of each joist. Cut a piece to length with tin snips when necessary. Decking is positioned on top of the joists as shown on pages 126–132. Fasteners are driven through holes in the metal track and into the boards (above, right). Work from underneath the deck, if possible, to avoid awkward positioning.

CHAPTER

7 BUILDING STAIRS AND RAMPS

tairs connect the deck to the surrounding landscape and join levels in multilevel decks. A stair may be a single step up to a low-level deck or a long flight of steps reaching a deck more than 8 feet above ground level. The basic stair principles and methods for making stringers shown on these pages are used for all stairs. Plan stair locations carefully to make the best use of space and traffic patterns (see pages 5–8). Check local code regulations for stair width, rise and run measurements (see page 10), and acceptable railings before finalizing your plans. For safety, consider installing solid risers when the rise between steps is more than 4 inches.

CHAPTER SEVEN PROJECTS

CLOSER LOOK

CALCULATING STAIR MEASUREMENTS

Transferring stairs from a building plan to the building site requires that you know the exact distances involved. Determine the height required for the stairs based on the structure you build. Measure from the top of the decking to ground level at the stair location (photo 1). Use the information on page 10 to calculate the distance from the deck to the end of the stair. Place a long straight board in the direction the stair will run and measure out this distance. Use a level to check ground slope relative to the bottom of the deck (photo 2). Then measure from the bottom of the board if the ground slopes away from the deck (photo 3). Add this measurement to the deck height measurement. Calculate the stair tread and riser measurements necessary to make the stair stringers (see page 138). Adjust the overall stair run and ending point of the stairs, if necessary.

MAKING STRINGERS

There are two types of stringers. Open stringers (see the Closer Look, page 143), also called cut stringers, have notches for steps cut into them. Step treads are attached to the notches. Closed stringers (page 142) use cleats attached to the inner faces to support the tread ends and provide an attractive smooth face for a stair run. See page 10 to determine the rise and run measurements

necessary to make both types of stringers. Choose the stringer type that best suits your deck design. Most codes allow only a 1/4-inch difference in height between the rise of each step. Plan carefully and remeasure before making stringers.

Plan to build deck stairs at least 3 feet wide for ease of traffic flow and safe use. Most codes require a 3-foot minimum stair width anyway. An additional stringer is installed between outer stringers for support. This stringer must be

an open stringer even if you use closed stringers for the outer ones. Install extra open stringers about every 16 inches on wider stairs when using 5/4-inch-thick lumber for treads and every 24 inches for 2× lumber.

Use the best 2×12 boards you can find for stringers. Open stringers must be made from pressure-treated lumber. Remember to apply preservative to the cut edges. Many codes allow wood other than pressure-treated for closed stringers.

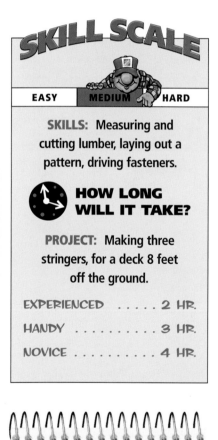

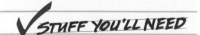

STUFF YOU'LL NEED

TOOLS: Tape measure, framing square, stair gauges, circular saw, jigsaw, drill, ratchet and socket.

MATERIALS: Lumber, fasteners.

OPEN STRINGERS

RUN

RISE

1   **CLAMP ONE STAIR GAUGE** (see page 139) onto the long leg of the square to set the tread run measurement. Place the gauge on the inside edge of the leg so it won't interfere with marking. Position it so the run measurement indicated by the scale on the outer edge of the leg intersects the edge of the board. If installing closed risers, allow for the thickness of the riser board when figuring the run measurement. Clamp the other gauge on the short leg for the rise distance.

OPEN STRINGERS (CONTINUED)

2 **MARK THE RISE AND RUN** for the first step at the top end of the stringer. Place the framing square on the board for the stringer with the gauges resting against what will be the top edge. Intersect the corner of the board with the rise line. The rise measurement at the top end of the stringer sets the stringer at the correct distance from the decking surface.

3 **EXTEND THE RISE LINE** to the bottom edge of the stringer. Mark an 'X' in waste areas to prevent confusion.

4 **MARK THE RISE AND RUN** for the next step. Slide the framing square down the stringer edge until the rise line touches the point where the tread line from the previous step intersects the board edge. Make certain the stair gauges rest against the board. Repeat this process to mark all steps.

STAIRS AND RAMPS

139

5 **PLACE THE FRAMING SQUARE** on the opposite edge of the board to mark the bottom end of the stringer. The stair gauges must rest against the board edge to maintain proper alignment. First extend the final rise line across the end of the board. Then mark a line the distance of the rise from the tread line on the last step.

6 **MARK ANOTHER LINE** above this last line. Make the distance between the lines equal to the thickness of the boards used for the stair treads. This line is the bottom of the stringer. Subtract the tread thickness from the first riser so the step up from the ground won't be too high.

7 **CUT THE TOP END** of the stringer at the extended rise line. Then make the top tread cut. Use a sharp blade in a circular saw to make crisp cuts with clean edges.

8 **MAKE THE CUT** for the riser to the top step. Stop the saw blade when it touches the tread line in the step corner. Then cut along the tread line. Stop the blade when it touches the riser line.

STAIRS AND RAMPS

9 **COMPLETE THE CUTS** in the step corner with a jigsaw, which has a thinner blade than a circular saw blade. Cut along the outside of the circular saw blade kerf to remove all the waste material.

10 **OPTION A:** Finish all of the step cuts. Make the cut for the bottom of the stringer. This completes the stringer if the bottom will be attached with brackets (see page 148).

10 **OPTION B:** Mark a notch in the bottom end of the stringer after finishing the cuts. The notch is for a toe kick used to attach the bottom end of the stringer (see page 148). Size the notch to fit over a horizontal 2×4 toe kick.

11 **USE THE COMPLETED STRINGER** as a template to mark boards for the remaining stringers. First hold the completed stringer in place to check for accuracy. Then clamp the template stringer to each board to make certain the marking is accurate.

CLOSED STRINGERS

TREAD THICKNESS

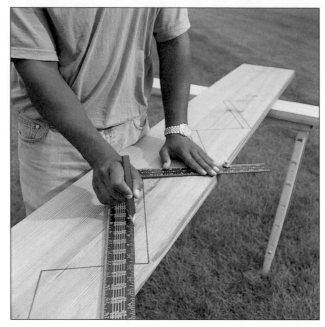

1 **USE A COMPLETED OPEN STRINGER** as a template to mark boards for closed stringers. Make the open stringer as shown (pages 138–141). An open stringer provides necessary support between closed stringers on deck stairs. Position the template with the step corners set back from the edge of a closed stringer board by the thickness of the treads.

2 **MARK THE TREAD POSITIONS** on the closed stringer. The complete outline is marked to make this clear. You only need to mark tread locations and the top and bottom ends of the stringer. Cut the extended riser line at the top end of the stringer to make the vertical edge for attaching the stringer to the deck. Then cut the bottom edge and final riser line at the bottom end of the stringer (see page 141).

3 **FASTEN A STAIR BRACKET** (see page 18) at each tread location on the closed stringers, using fasteners recommended by the manufacturer. Align the top surface of the horizontal flange on a cleat with the bottom edge of the tread location. Attach cleats either before or after the stringer is installed.

4 **ATTACH A STAIR BRACKET** at each tread location on the open stringers. Screws or nails may be driven through treads into open stringers, but using cleats provides an invisible connection similar to that on closed stringers. Align the top surface of the cleat with the edge of the stringer. Install cleats on opposite sides of the stringer for adjacent tread locations.

5 **DRIVE FASTENERS** recommended by the manufacturer (usually short lag screws) through the cleats into the undersides of the treads. Use a driver attachment in your drill that fits the lag screw heads.

6 **USE A RATCHET** and an appropriate-size socket to drive fasteners in spaces too small to use the drill.

CLOSER LOOK

FINAL TREAD TREATMENTS

Treads may be installed with the ends overlapping the outer edges of open stringers by 1 inch (below, left), which is an attractive alternative to installing the ends flush with the outer edges.

Round over the edges of the treads with a power sander, such as a random orbital sander (below, right). Notch the end of a tread when installing a railing post, if necessary.

BUILDING TRADITIONAL STAIRS

Traditional stairs require at least three stringers (for a 3-foot-wide stair). The two outer stringers are either open or closed stringers, depending on the style you choose. Center stringers are always open stringers. Install more center stringers for stairs wider than 3 feet (see page 138).

Use a landing to break up a long stair run to make using the stairs easier and safer. Also use a landing to change the direction of the stair run. Rise and run measurements must stay the same for the stair runs above and below the landing. Install permanent bracing for small landings to provide stability.

Make treads from separate pieces of decking material. Remember to place a gap between board pieces. Two 6-inch wide boards with a 1/4-inch gap fit an 11-inch tread run. Or cut treads from solid lumber, such as a 2×12.

The stair run in this project has a landing that separates it into an upper and lower run at right angles to each other. The outer stringers are closed stringers. Follow the instructions for the lower stair run for stairs that don't need a landing.

SKILL SCALE

EASY — **MEDIUM** — HARD

SKILLS: Measuring and layout, digging and pouring footings, cutting lumber, driving fasteners.

HOW LONG WILL IT TAKE?

PROJECT: Building stairs with one landing.

EXPERIENCED . . . . . . 1 DAY

HANDY . . . . 1.5 DAYS

NOVICE . . . . 2 DAYS

✔ STUFF YOU'LL NEED

TOOLS: Tape measure, line level, water level, chalk line, shovel, power auger, posthole digger, maul, hammer, masonry finishing tools, speed square, circular saw, jigsaw, drill, ratchet and socket.

MATERIALS: Lumber, fasteners, spikes, premixed concrete, angle brackets, skewable joist hangers, stair cleats.

1 **INSTALL AND TRIM DECKING** at the portion of the deck where stairs attach. Lay out stair footing and pad positions (see pages 76–77) after completing the deck framing. Use the information on page 10 to determine these positions. Dig and pour the footings and pad (see pages 78–81).

2 **INSTALL POSTS** for the stair landing (see pages 91–93). Leave temporary bracing in place until permanent braces are installed.

3 **DRILL PILOT HOLES** and attach rim joists to the outside of the posts with lag screws or carriage bolts (see page 16). The top of the landing is essentially a step within the stair run. Position top edges of the joists so the decking will be at a height equivalent to a tread in the stair run.

4 **INSTALL PERMANENT DIAGONAL BRACES** on the inside of the posts (see page 108). Attach braces made from 6-inch-wide lumber, to two adjacent sides of the landing. Measure and cut each brace so the ends are flush with the outside post faces.

5 **ATTACH DECKING** after installing joists (see pages 109–115). Align decking to match the pattern used on the main deck, if possible. Perpendicular decking usually is aligned with the length of a landing; the joists are installed across the shortest landing dimension.

STAIRS AND RAMPS

6 **MEASURE BETWEEN A PLUMB LINE** at the edge of the deck and the facing edge of the landing. Check this distance after the landing is built in case its position shifts during construction. Also check the distance between the landing and the concrete pad for the bottom end of the stairs. Adjust rise and run measurements, if necessary.

7 **MAKE STRINGERS** for the lower stairs following the methods shown on pages 138–142. Cut notches in the bottom ends of the stringers if you will attach them to the pad with a toe kick (see the Closer Look Tip on page 148.) Complete one open stringer and use it as a template for the other stringers for accurate construction.

8 **ATTACH 2x4 CLEATS** to the backside of the rim joist facing the concrete pad. The cleats will support a nailer that provides a surface to attach the top ends of the stringers (see Step 10). Measure the top end of a stringer, add ½ inch (so the nailer will extend beneath the stringer), and add this length to the rise measurement. Position the bottom edge of the nailer at this combined distance from the decking. Cut and install cleats, bottom ends flush with the bottom edge of the nailer.

OOPS!

I thought I was careful enough when I laid out footing locations and built the landing for my deck stairs. When I began making stringers, I realized the landing location was too narrow on one side by over one inch. Fortunately I realized that I could attach another layer of rim joist on that side. I had to replace the decking; but once I did, it was almost impossible to tell that I had even made a mistake!

STAIRS AND RAMPS

9 **FASTEN THE NAILER** to the cleats with deck screws. Cut the nailer to length and width from 2× pressure-treated lumber. Install a nailer for the upper stair run using the same method.

10 **ATTACH EACH CENTER STRINGER** with a skewable joist hanger (see page 18). Level the tops of the center stringers.

11 **CONNECT EACH OUTER STRINGER** to the landing with an angle bracket (see page 18). Align the top tread location on a closed stringer with the top edge of an open stringer.

12 **MARK THE LOCATION** for the bottom end of each stringer on the concrete pad. Use a framing square to align the stringers with the landing.

STAIRS AND RAMPS

13 **FASTEN AN ANGLE BRACKET** to the pad with self-tapping masonry screws. Drill pilot holes in the pad with a masonry bit. Drive nails recommended by the bracket manufacturer through the bracket and into the stringer.

14 **DRIVE SHORT LAG SCREWS** through stair cleats (see page 16) into the back sides of the treads. Cut treads from the same wood as the decking. Attach stair cleats for closed stringers as shown on page 142. Stair cleats also can be used on open stringers if you want an invisible connection. Or drive screws or nails through the treads into the top edges of open stringers.

NAILER

15 **MARK THE LOCATION** of the front edge of the bottom end of each outer stringer for the upper stair run. Make stringers as you did for the lower stair run. Temporarily position each outer stringer to mark its location. Check alignment to the deck with a framing square. Snap a chalk line across the landing at the marks.

CLOSER LOOK

ADDING A TOE KICK

A toe kick is an option for attaching the bottom ends of stringers to a concrete pad. Check local codes to determine how thick the pad must be. Make the toe kick from 2×4 pressure-treated lumber. Fasten it to the pad with the same type of threaded rods, nuts, and washers used to attach post anchors to footings (see page 89). Epoxy bonds the rods into holes drilled in the pad. Cure fresh concrete for at least 48 hours before installing the rods.

16 **ATTACH A TOE KICK,** made from a pressure-treated 2×4, to the landing with deck screws. Align its front edge with the chalk line. Cut it to a length that will fit between the outer stringers. Outer stringers also can be notched to fit over a toe kick, but this is usually less attractive.

17 **CUT A NOTCH** in the bottom end of the center stringer sized to fit over the toe kick.

18 **ATTACH EACH OUTER STRINGER** to the deck with angle brackets. Install the center stringer in a skewable joist hanger.

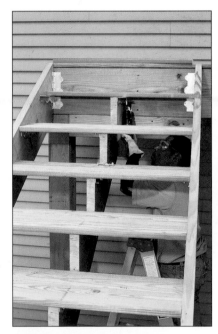

19 **DRIVE TWO DECK SCREWS** through each outer stringer into an end of the toe kick. Drill pilot holes for the screws to prevent splitting the wood. Drill pilot holes for these screws, then toenail the center stringer to the toe kick with deck screws.

20 **ATTACH STAIR CLEATS** to the stringers as you did for the lower stair run.

21 **DRIVE FASTENERS** through the cleats and into the undersides of the treads. The stairs and landing are now ready for railings.

WRAPPING STAIRS AROUND A CORNER

Building stairs that wrap around a corner is usually done on decks less than 4 feet high. Open stringers (see page 138) are required for this stair style with a stringer that projects out from the corner. Tread run dimensions on the corner stringer must be longer than the run dimensions on the other stringers. Longer dimensions are necessary because 45-degree mitered ends of treads meet over the corner stringer. An end cut at 45 degrees is longer than one cut at 90 degrees. Treads made from 5/4×6 lumber are installed on two-step stringers in this project.

CORNER STRINGER WILL BE PLACED HERE

SKILL SCALE

EASY　**MEDIUM**　HARD

SKILLS: Measuring and cutting lumber, laying out a pattern, driving fasteners.

HOW LONG WILL IT TAKE?

PROJECT: Wrapping stairs with three steps around one corner.

EXPERIENCED . . . . . 2 HR.

HANDY . . . . 3.5 HR.

NOVICE . . . . 5 HR.

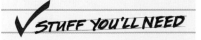
✔ STUFF YOU'LL NEED

TOOLS: Tape measure, speed square, level, framing square, stair gauges, circular saw, jigsaw, drill.

MATERIALS: Lumber, fasteners.

1 INSTALL A STRINGER (see page 138) on each side of the deck corner. Make one face of each stringer flush with the corner. Space the remaining stringers on both sides of the deck according to the tread thickness you will use (see page 138). Anchor the bottom ends of the stringers with toe kicks (see page 148).

TREADS POSITIONED TEMPORARILY

2 MAKE THE FIRST MEASUREMENT for the corner stringer. Cut a 45-degree miter at one end of two tread pieces. Temporarily position the treads on the stringers at the corner to rest against the upper risers with the mitered ends together. Measure between the corner made by the two end stringers and the inside corner of the intersecting treads.

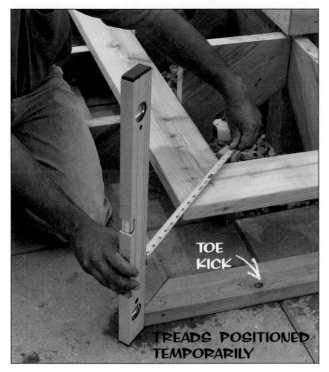

TOE KICK

TREADS POSITIONED TEMPORARILY

3 **MAKE THE SECOND MEASUREMENT** for the corner stringer. Plumb a level against the outside corner of the toe-kick intersection. Measure between the inside edge of the level and the inside corner of the intersecting treads. Note: This measurement will be for all remaining tread runs on stringers with more than two treads.

5 **ATTACH TREADS** with mitered ends meeting at the corner stringer. Center the end of a board over the stringer edge. Install the corner stringer with toenailed screws. Drill pilot holes for fasteners to prevent splitting.

45° BEVEL

4 **MAKE THE CORNER STRINGER.** The upper tread run is equal to the measurement from Step 2. The lower tread run is equal to the measurement from Step 3. Cut a 45-degree bevel on both sides of the stringer end so it won't stick out past the toe kick (see Step 5). Cut a 5-inch-long notch to fit over the toe-kick intersection.

BUYER'S GUIDE

SIMPLIFY WITH PRECUT STRINGERS

Precut open stringers in various sizes, available at many home building centers, can simplify stair installation if you find a size that fits your deck. Check each stringer for defects before purchasing.

Designer Tip

STAIR STYLES TO FIT YOUR DESIGN

Build the same style of stairs between several deck levels to visually connect the levels. Use a different stair style to emphasize distinct areas. Stairs that are built across the full width of the area between deck levels make the levels flow together, and provide a smooth transition between a low-level deck and the surrounding landscape.

BUILDING AN ACCESS RAMP

An access ramp provides a more comfortable way to change levels for people who can't climb stairs. This includes people who use canes and walkers as well as wheelchairs.

Locate a ramp at a doorway that provides the most convenient and acceptable access. Position a landing in front of the doorway. If the door opens toward the landing, allow at least 4 feet beyond the open door. Also, direct roof runoff away from the ramp area with a gutter.

Build an access ramp with the same methods used to build a deck, including stair layout and building techniques. The only differences are: The "deck platform" of the ramp is sloped and stringers supporting a ramp section that reaches ground level are tapered. Leave a $1/8$-inch gap between decking boards so water drains from the ramp surface.

The concrete transition at the end of the ramp (page 154) may crack over time and require patching. An option is to install a piece of aluminum diamond plate as the transition between ramp and pad.

The maximum allowable slope is 1 inch of rise for every 12 inches of run (called 1-in-12 slope). A more gradual slope may be necessary for some ramps. Minimum ramp width is 36 inches but a 42- to 48-inch-wide ramp is usually best for wheelchair access. Railings or curbs are often required. Railings should have a graspable handrail (see page 156). A curb is a piece of wood installed at an outer ramp edge that is at least 2 inches higher than the ramp surface. Check with local code for specific access ramp regulations in your area.

Cut stringers for ramps that are less than 10 feet long from boards wide enough to eliminate the need for posts. Support the ground-level end of the ramp with a concrete pad or sidewalk. Longer ramps require footings and posts to support stringers and landings (see page 76). The ramp to the 8-inch-high deck in this project is 96 inches long (a 1-in-12 slope).

SKILL SCALE

EASY · **MEDIUM** · HARD

SKILLS: Measuring and marking a pattern, cutting lumber, driving fasteners, installing concrete.

HOW LONG WILL IT TAKE?

PROJECT: Building a 10-foot-long access ramp. Does not include drying time.

EXPERIENCED . . . . . . 6 HR.

HANDY . . . . 8 HR.

NOVICE . . . . 10 HR.

✓ STUFF YOU'LL NEED

TOOLS: Tape measure, speed square, straightedge, maul, circular saw, jigsaw, drill, masonry tools.

MATERIALS: Lumber, fasteners, premixed concrete, joist hangers.

LANDING

PAD

RAMP

1 **MEASURE BETWEEN THE DECK** and the concrete pad or sidewalk and mark the end point of the ramp. First measure the height of the deck surface from ground level. Then calculate the run length necessary for the deck height. Note: See pages 76–81 for information on installing a concrete pad if one doesn't exist at your site.

2 **MAKE AND USE ONE STRINGER** as a template to mark boards for the others. Lay out the rise and run slope on one board. Make the narrow tip of the stringer 1½ inches high. Mark a ¾×4-inch notch in the bottom edge of the narrow end to fit over a cleat. Remove the notch with a jigsaw and make long cuts with a circular saw. Then use this stringer as a template.

1½ IN.

3 **CUT A 1½-INCH-WIDE STRIP** from 1×6 pressure-treated lumber. First adjust the blade angle on the circular saw and cut a 5-degree bevel on one edge of the board. Then cut the strip so the widest face is equal to 1½ inches. Make the strip as long as the ramp is wide.

cut the 5° bevel on this edge first

Designer Tip

RAMP LANDINGS

Include a landing in an access ramp that rises more than 3 feet so you have a resting place within a long run. Make the landing at least 4 feet long. A landing where turning is required should be 5 feet long. Construct long ramps along the length of a deck.

4 **FASTEN THE STRINGERS** to a cleat attached to the concrete pad or sidewalk. The cleat is the piece of pressure-treated 1×6 remaining from Step 3. Attach the cleat to concrete with the same type of threaded rods, nuts, and washers used for attaching post anchors to footings (see page 89). Install the stringers in joist hangers attached to the deck.

5 **ATTACH THE 1½-INCH-WIDE STRIP** to the ends of the stringers with the widest face against the stringers. Drill pilot holes for the fasteners to prevent splitting.

6 **FASTEN THE TREAD** to the narrow end of the stringers to overlap the strip about 1 inch. Install the remaining treads with ⅛-inch gaps between them, if necessary (see page 125).

7 **SMOOTH CONCRETE** poured to make a transition from the ramp to the pad or sidewalk. Apply a bonding agent over existing concrete. Make certain concrete fills the space under the lip of the final tread. See pages 69–81 for more information on working with concrete. (Use waste pieces remaining from cutting the stringers as forms for the concrete. These pieces already have the proper slope.)

RAILINGS

Most decks and stairs need a railing. For example, most codes require a deck with more than two steps to have a railing and second-story decks to have a 42-inch tall railing. Check local code to determine railing requirements for your deck. Balusters must be spaced close enough together so that a 4-inch sphere cannot pass through. Pay particular attention to spacing for milled balusters. Balusters should run vertically; codes do not allow horizontal balusters because children can use them as a ladder to climb over the railing.

Choose a railing style (page 156) that complements your house, deck, and landscape. Decide on a style before you install decking since some railing posts must be attached before decking. When you install a railing, your deck is probably almost completed, and you might be tempted to work quickly. But work carefully because the railing is one of the most visible parts of the deck.

RAILINGS

CHAPTER EIGHT PROJECTS

Designer Tip

RAILING OPTIONS TO COMPLEMENT A DECK

A wide variety of post, rail, and baluster styles are available that can be used with any railing style (see below). Choose those that best complement the deck design and other decorative elements of your house and landscape.

Railing posts usually are made from 4×4 lumber in several lengths. The standard post has flat faces throughout. Milled posts have decorative profiles cut in their faces. Or you can cut a profile into a standard square post if you have basic woodworking tools and skills. A separate post cap or finial (a decorative knob-like attachment) can be attached to the top of a standard post.

Besides basic 2×4 and 2×6 rail arrangements, rails are available with milled decorative profiles.

Choose one that matches the post and baluster style. Milled rails are usually precut to fit over a 2×2. Graspable handrails are often required on stairs by local code. Code may specify maximum dimensions for the size of the handrail.

Standard balusters with flat faces are made from 2×2 lumber. Some have a precut mitered end. Several decorative profiles are available in milled balusters. Another popular type is made from coated metal tubing (see pages 168–170).

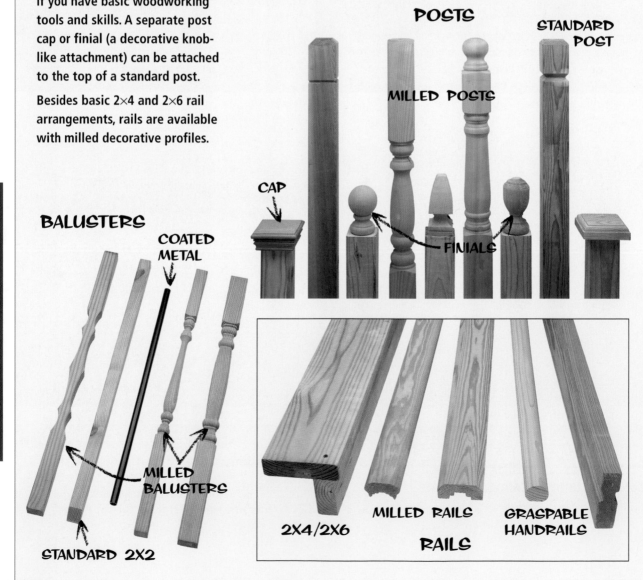

POSTS

STANDARD POST

MILLED POSTS

CAP

FINIALS

BALUSTERS

COATED METAL

MILLED BALUSTERS

STANDARD 2X2

2X4/2X6

MILLED RAILS

GRASPABLE HANDRAILS

RAILS

MARK A THROUGH POST at the correct height for the railing (see page 162). Level a mason's string line between posts or use a water level. Remember that the trimming height for the post depends on whether the post protrudes above the top rail or is covered by a cap rail.

CUT IDENTICALLY SPACED NOTCHES in posts by clamping them together, called ganging, before cutting. Ganging is a quicker method than cutting post notches one at a time. Properly align the post ends before clamping them together.

CAP RAIL OR PROTRUDING POSTS

Post tops can be covered by a top horizontal rail, a cap rail (near left), which makes a smooth, uninterrupted railing line around the deck. Cap rails are a common treatment when posts pass through the deck from the footings. The other option is to let post tops protrude above the top rail (far right). Milled posts or decorative caps or finials are often used in this style. Milled posts usually aren't long enough to pass through from the footings unless they're installed on a low-level deck. In that case, use pressure-treated lumber for the milled posts.

You may want to install a small support block for longer railing spans.

RAILINGS

ATTACH ADDITIONAL POSTS between through posts so they are in line with the through posts. Do this before installing the decking. Install additional posts at the inside face of the header joist in a corner where a joist meets the header joist, if possible (above, left). Otherwise, fasten it to the header joist. Install additional posts at the inside face of the rim joist. Install blocking to provide adequate support for the post (above, right). Fasten a post with carriage bolts.

INSTALL A NOTCHED RAILING POST around a deck corner (above, left). This saves the cost and time of installing one post on each side of the corner (see page 159). Cutting this type of notch is more complicated than notches cut across the face of a post (see page 97). Rails also must be attached in a notch on this type of post installation (above, right). Mark and cut the notch following the same techniques used for the notch at the bottom of the post. Cut a 45-degree bevel in the end of each rail. Drill pilot holes and drive deck screws at an angle to fasten the rails in the notch.

RAILINGS

ATTACH ONE POST on each side of a deck corner when installing posts without notches. Space the posts about a baluster's width apart. Fasten the rails to the inner post faces. Use a butt joint where the rails meet in the corner.

CUT A 45-DEGREE BEVEL at the bottom end of each post to provide an attractive transition between the bottoms of the posts and the perimeter joist. Make the bevel as large as you wish and be consistent. Bevels can be cut on posts without notches or posts with notches.

SCARF JOINT ADDS STRENGTH WHERE NEEDED

Join two rail pieces that attach to the face of a post with a scarf joint (near left) for a stronger joint than a butt joint. Cut opposing 45-degree bevels in the ends of the rail pieces. Center the joint on the post face. Note: The length of a 45-degree beveled cut in a 2× board is 1½ inches. Use this measurement when you figure necessary rail lengths. Drill pilot holes and drive fasteners at an angle through the joint to attach the rail pieces. Use a butt joint between rail pieces installed in a notch because the notch provides strong support. Make the outer face of each rail flush with a perimeter joist face if balusters will be attached to the perimeter joists (above, right). For example, fasten rails to inner faces of posts installed without notches for the balusters to be vertical.

INSTALLING RAILINGS

Install railings on decks more than 30 inches higher than ground level. Local codes regulate minimum railing height; however, 36 inches is common. Railing posts can be attached to the outer face of the perimeter joists or be through posts (passing through the deck from the footings). Usually additional posts must be installed between through posts. Attach rails to either type of railing post using the methods shown here.

Use any railing style that meets code (page 156). Spacing between balusters and between lower rails and decking can be no more than 4 inches (page 155). Plan spacing carefully if you choose balusters with decorative profiles because uneven surfaces may create larger spaces. Stairs with four or more steps must have a railing on at least one side. Stair railing can match the rest of the deck railing and must meet local code minimum height regulations. Graspable handrails attached to the inside of stair railings may be required. Handrail height should be between 30 and 34 inches above the treads. Many codes also require a handrail return (see page 166) at the upper end of a handrail.

Pages 160–166 show a railing project with rails attached to posts in notches. The same angles and basic methods are used if rails are attached to post faces. This railing also has two rails, but balusters could attach to perimeter joists. The metal baluster railing on pages 168–170 shows rails attached between post faces. The metal balusters (usually aluminum) require two rails and are coated with a baked-enamel finish. They are precut to lengths for standard railing heights.

SKILL SCALE

EASY · **MEDIUM** · HARD

SKILLS: Measuring and cutting lumber, driving fasteners.

HOW LONG WILL IT TAKE?

PROJECT: Installing a railing on a 16×12-foot deck.

EXPERIENCED . . . . . 10 HR.

HANDY . . . . 12 HR.

NOVICE . . . . 14 HR.

✔ STUFF YOU'LL NEED

TOOLS: Tape measure, level, clamp, chisel, hammer, power miter saw, drill.

MATERIALS: Lumber, fasteners, handrail support brackets.

1 **MEASURE THE EXACT DIMENSION** of each railing run. A railing run is a straight section of railing uninterrupted by stairs or other changes in direction. Use the information on page 9 to calculate the number and location of posts, and the gap between balusters for each run.

RAILINGS

2 **PLUMB AND ATTACH EACH POST** with two carriage bolts or lag screws. Stagger the fasteners on both sides of the center of the post to prevent splitting, and align the stagger in the same direction on each post for an attractive appearance. Cut notches in posts before attaching, if necessary for the railing style. Make notches for rails the same depth as the bottom notches.

3 **FASTEN EACH RAIL** to the posts. Drill pilot holes for fasteners at the ends of each rail to prevent splitting.

4 **MARK THE SLANTED TOP SHOULDER** of a notch for a post that will attach to a stair stringer. Plumb the post against the stringer at its correct height before marking. Cut the notch and install the post. Position one post at each end of a stair run. Install additional posts for long stair runs (see page 11) or to match the railing design.

5 **MARK THE LOCATION** for the upper edge of the top rail or for trimming the post top, depending on the railing style. Lay a long straight 2×4 across the stair treads. Measure between 34 and 38 inches from the bottom edge of the 2×4 at each post to mark the top edge of a stair railing.

6 **MARK THE NOTCHES** for each stair rail in the posts. Hold or clamp the rails in position against the posts.

7 **MARK CUTTING LINES** on the end of the stair rail. End the rail in the center of the post if it meets a deck rail at the post. Also mark the stair rail notch location on the post. The post shown is trimmed to proper height.

CLOSER LOOK

STRONG JOINTS DON'T COME EASY

One method to make a joint between a stair rail and a deck rail is to center the joint in a notch in the post (below, left). This makes a very strong joint; however, the complex shape of the notch makes it more complicated to cut. Notice how the tip of the stair rail must be trimmed to make the end of the stair rail even with a square cut end of a deck rail. The other option is to attach only the deck rail in a straight notch. The straight notch is easier to cut, but the stair rail must be toenailed to the end of the deck rail (far right). Matching angles are cut in the ends of the stair and deck rails (see Step 14) and do not create as strong a joint as one supported by a notch.

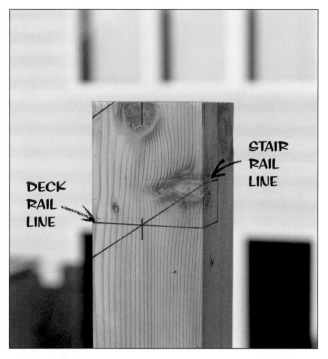

8 **MARK THE NOTCH LOCATION** for a deck rail that meets a stair rail at a post. The top of a post where stair rail and deck rail meet will be level with other posts for the deck railing.

9 **CUT THE NOTCH IN THE POST.** Remove as much of the notch as possible with a circular saw (see page 95). Then finish removing waste material with a chisel.

10 **MARK THE INTERSECTING ANGLE** between the stair rail and deck rail. Place the edge of the deck rail on the decking with one end protruding over the stairs. Lay the stair rail on edge on the treads to cross the deck rail. Mark both edges on both rails where they cross. Connect the marks across the face of each rail. Align a power miter saw blade with a marked line and cut each rail to length.

WORK SMARTER

CUT IT TWICE TO TEST BLADE ANGLE

Make the first cut for an unknown angle about $1/8$ inch from the marked line. This will determine whether the power miter saw blade is aligned correctly. Adjust the blade angle if there is an uneven space between the line and the kerf.

Then make the final cut. Making the first cut a short distance away from the line prevents cutting a rail too short with a misaligned blade.

11 **ATTACH THE STAIR RAILS** to the posts. Drill pilot holes at the ends of each rail to prevent splitting.

12 **INSTALL EACH BALUSTER** with two fasteners at each end. Check the distance between posts to make certain that the gap calculated in Step 1 is correct. Cut a spacer long enough to span between rails and as wide as the gap between balusters. Cut the tops of balusters for a stair railing at the proper angle before installing. Check plumb every fourth baluster. **Note: Balusters also may be attached after the cap rail is installed.**

Designer Tip

RAILING DESIGN

Make a unique focal point in a railing with a special baluster design, such as this simple sunburst pattern. Special designs have to comply with the maximum allowable space between balusters.

13 **ATTACH CAP RAIL** across the tops of the posts and balusters. Cap rail is usually made from 2×6 lumber. Make a scarf joint (see page 159) to join pieces of cap rail for a long railing. Center the joint over a post and drive two fasteners into posts. Drive one fastener every 12-16 inches between posts into rails and balusters.

RAILINGS

14 **DRIVE FASTENERS** through the cap rail into posts at each corner. Cut a 45-degree miter in the ends of cap-rail pieces that meet in a 90-degree corner. Also drive a fastener through the outside corner of the miter joint from both directions to keep the joint tight.

15 **TEMPORARILY POSITION A CAP-RAIL BOARD** over an upper stair rail. Rough-cut the board a few inches longer than finished length. Hold the board to mark the angle where it meets the post. Cut the bevel in the end of the board (see Tip on page 166).

16 **DRIVE FASTENERS** at an angle through the beveled end of the cap rail and into the post. Drill pilot holes to prevent splitting.

17 **ATTACH A GRASPABLE HANDRAIL** to the inside, or top, of a stair railing, if necessary. Use brass, galvanized, or other rust-resistant stair rail hardware. Smooth any sharp edges on the handrail with sandpaper.

18 **FASTEN A HANDRAIL RETURN,** if required. Miter the ends of the handrail pieces at 45 degrees, which may take trial and error on some railing profiles. Cut and test-fit the pieces before attaching them.

Designer Tip

INSTALLING CAP RAILS

Install upper and lower rails and the cap rail between post faces if post tops protrude above rails in the railing design. Attach the rails to post faces with toenailed screws. Or install rails on small metal angle brackets (see page 169).

CLOSER LOOK

CUTTING
COMPOUND ANGLES

Attaching an angled stair rail to a deck rail post (below, left) requires cutting a compound angle in the end of the stair rail. A compound angle requires cutting a bevel angle and a miter angle simultaneously; it's easiest to do with a compound miter saw (below, right). A circular saw also will make this cut, but it is more difficult to control accurately. It often takes trial and error to make a tight fit between rail and post. Rough-cut the rail to length 1 foot longer than necessary. Cut the opposite end to final length once an accurate compound angle is made. Or determine accurate angles with test cuts in scrap rail pieces.

RAILINGS FOR STAIRS AT A 45-DEGREE ANGLE TO DECK

1 **INSTALL A STAIR RAILING POST** at the top end of an angled stair stringer. Make a space between the post and the deck rail post no wider than the spacing between balusters. Also install the stair railing post at the bottom end of the stringer.

2 **MARK THE ANGLE** for trimming each stair rail. Measure and mark locations for rail height (see page 160). Temporarily position each stair rail board against the stair rail posts at the marks to mark the trimming line at each end of the board.

3 **CUT THE MITER** at both ends of each stair rail (see Work Smarter Tip on page 163).

4 **INSTALL THE STAIR RAILS,** balusters, and cap rail following the methods used on the deck railing.

RAILING WITH COATED METAL BALUSTERS

1 **ATTACH RAILING POSTS** following the method used on traditional railings (see page 157). Space posts as evenly as possible for each straight section of railing. Measure and cut pairs of 2×4 rails to length. Rails can be attached between post faces or in notches cut in the post faces.

2 **MARK HOLE LOCATIONS** for the ³/4-inch-diameter balusters 4¹/2 inches apart on center. (Space between balusters will be 3³/4 inches.) Make a 2×4 story pole longer than the rails with this spacing marked on its edge. Begin marks at the center point of the 2×4. Clamp a rail pair to the story pole. Align the center point of the rail pair with that on the story pole. Slide the rails over 2¹/4 inches if hole locations are within 1¹/2 inches of the ends. Use a speed square to mark locations accurately.

3 **DRILL A ³/4-INCH-DIAMETER HOLE** that is ³/4 inch deep at each mark. Use a portable drill guide (see page 23) to make holes consistently vertical. Use a Forstner bit to cut the holes (see Tool Tip, right).

TOOL TIP

DRILL THE RIGHT HOLE

Where appearance is important, drill holes with a Forstner bit. This bit cuts a hole with a crisp edge. A spade bit usually cuts a hole with a more ragged edge. Use a spade bit when drilling holes for carriage bolts and lag screws.

RAILINGS

4 **INSERT A BALUSTER** in each hole in the bottom rail after applying a small amount of silicone caulk in each hole. The caulk helps prevent moisture penetration. Wear gloves when using silicone.

5 **FIT THE TOP RAIL** over the ends of the balusters. Lay a piece of 1x lumber under the balusters to raise the ends and to assist with the assembling. Brace the bottom rail to keep it from moving, and stand the assembly upright. Hammer against a scrap wood block placed on the top rail to completely seat both ends of the balusters in the rails.

 WORK SMARTER

STRONG BRACKETS

Small angle brackets make a strong and easy connection when attaching rails between post faces. Fasten the brackets to the post faces at the proper heights. Position one bracket underneath each rail end location. Set the rails onto the brackets. Drive screws through the brackets into the rails and toenail a screw through the top edge of each rail.

6 **INSTALL EACH RAIL ASSEMBLY** between the appropriate posts.

7 **ATTACH CAP RAIL** over the top rail. Join cap rail pieces with a scarf joint centered over a post (see page 159). Make 45-degree miter joints at the corners (see page 165).

8 **DRILL HOLES** for stair rail balusters with the rails resting on the stair treads. Cut the rails to length with the ends trimmed at the proper angle. Turn the top rail 180 degrees and flip it upside down before clamping the rails together. Mark hole locations 5 1/2 inches on center. (Mark the other edge of the story pole.) Use a level to plumb the portable drill guide, if necessary.

RAILINGS

9 **ASSEMBLE AND INSTALL** the stair rail sections with the same methods used for the deck railing.

Designer Tip

RAILING APPEAL

Centerpieces, in various styles and matching colors, attach to metal balusters easily with screws provided by the manufacturer. Finials for post tops also are available.

CHAPTER 9

BUILDING DECK ACCESSORIES

Accessories customize a deck to suit your needs. Many accessories may be added after you use the deck for a while and determine what will be most useful. However, some projects must be planned before the deck is built. Portions of built-in benches, privacy screens, and arbors often require installation during deck building. Low-voltage lighting also is easier to install while framing a low-level deck. Installing lighting for a raised deck often is simpler after the deck is built. Check with local code for regulations concerning your accessory projects.

DECK ACCESSORIES

ATTACHING SKIRTING AND FASCIA

Attach skirting if you want to cover the open area underneath the deck. Install lattice made from the same type of wood used on the deck. Lattice is the least expensive skirting material and provides good support for climbing plants. You may want to back lattice with netting to prevent small animals from getting under your deck. Or build skirting from siding material that matches your house. This usually requires more framing installation than lattice skirting. Install access panels in skirting for storage areas underneath a deck. Low-level decks generally don't need skirting because the natural ground cover and landscaping conceal the space.

Attach fascia boards to cover pressure-treated lumber used for deck framing. Make fascia from the same type of wood used for the decking and railing, such as cedar or redwood. Attach skirting to the back of fascia if fascia that is wider than the rim joist is installed. Fascia also may be installed to cover the ends of decking boards; however, this method may trap moisture and hasten wood deterioration in damp climates. Installing fascia usually is not worth the extra expense and time if you will apply paint or an opaque stain, or let lumber weather to a natural gray.

SKILL SCALE

EASY **MEDIUM** HARD

SKILLS: Measuring and cutting lumber and lattice, driving fasteners.

HOW LONG WILL IT TAKE?

PROJECT: Attaching skirting and fascia to a 16×12-foot deck.

EXPERIENCED . . . . . . 1 HR.

HANDY . . . . 1.5 HR.

NOVICE . . . . 2 HR.

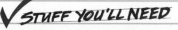

✔ *STUFF YOU'LL NEED*

TOOLS: Tape measure, straightedge, maul, hammer, nail set, circular saw, drill.

MATERIALS: Lumber, lattice, rebar, fasteners, hinge and hook hardware.

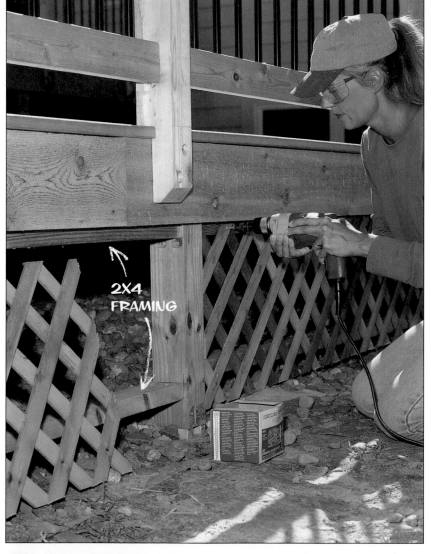

1 **ATTACH SKIRTING** to the deck posts with short deck screws after drilling pilot holes to prevent splitting. Install additional 2×4 framing between posts to support the edges of the skirting material. Cut lattice to size with a circular saw guided by a long straightedge. Wear eye protection when cutting.

DECK ACCESSORIES

172

2 **DRILL HOLES FOR SPIKES** or 12-inch lengths of rebar through framing resting on the ground. Install pressure-treated framing at ground level where there aren't posts. Make a flat area underneath the framing. Drive spikes or rebar through the holes to anchor framing to the ground.

3 **MAKE ACCESS PANELS** for storage areas underneath the deck. Hinges aren't necessary. Just install sliding bolts or hook-and-eye hardware to hold the panel in place. Use brass or other rust-resistant hardware. Attach 1× lumber frames around each skirting section if desired.

CLOSER LOOK

ATTACHING FASCIA

Fasten fascia to framing with galvanized finish or spiral shank nails (near left). Deck screws aren't necessary, and nails are less noticeable. Fascia is usually made from 1× lumber, but 2× lumber also can be used. Measure, cut, and install fascia pieces with mitered ends around corners (far right). Drive nails through the mitered joint from both directions to keep the joint tight. Use a nail set to drive nailheads flush with the wood surface to prevent the hammer from making dimples in the fascia.

BUILDING BENCHES

enches are either freestanding or built-in. Freestanding benches can be moved according to need. Built-in benches are fastened to joists or railing posts. Install built-in benches at the perimeter of a low-level deck that doesn't require a railing to help define the edge of the deck and to form a barrier. On higher decks, be careful where you place freestanding benches so children don't use them to climb over a railing. Built-in benches on a deck that requires a railing must have a railing that extends 36 inches from the top of the bench. To gain storage, enclose the area beneath a bench seat.

Build benches from 2× or larger lumber for stability and length between supports. Typical seat height for a bench is 15 to18 inches. Seat depth is usually at least 15 inches but may be as much as 30 inches. The bench projects beginning on this page are 5 feet long. The seats are 18 inches high and 17 inches wide. To provide a smooth seating surface, sand all surfaces and round over sharp corners and edges.

Shown here are two bench projects among many types and styles. Use dimensions that suit your needs or pattern benches after one you see in a picture or on a deck. Benches complement your deck best when made from the same type of wood used for the decking and railing.

SKILL SCALE

EASY | MEDIUM | HARD

SKILLS: Measuring and marking a pattern, cutting and notching lumber, driving fasteners.

HOW LONG WILL IT TAKE?

PROJECT: Building one 5-foot-long bench.

EXPERIENCED . . . . . 4 HR.

HANDY . . . . 5 HR.

NOVICE . . . . 6 HR.

✔ STUFF YOU'LL NEED

TOOLS: Tape measure, speed square, clamps, chisel, circular saw, drill.

MATERIALS: Lumber, fasteners.

BUILDING A FREESTANDING BENCH

1 **MARK THE LAYOUT** for a pedestal (see step 4) on a 16-inch-long 4×4. Space notches 1½ inches apart. Mark a 45-degree bevel on each end that is 1 inch from the outer shoulders of the notches. Cut 3½-inch-wide by 1½-inch-deep notches with a circular saw (see page 95). Remove waste material from the notches with a chisel (shown).

2 **CUT A 45-DEGREE SHOULDER** at both ends of the long notch on the bottom side of each bottom pedestal. Angle the cuts toward each other. The bottom edges of the kerfs should be 1/2 inch below the face of the 4×4. Remove the remainder of the notch as in Step 1. Then cut the bevels on the ends of each pedestal.

3 **ATTACH THE 2×6 SPREADER** to the inside surface of a 4×4 leg at each end of the bench. Drive three deck screws at each end. Install one 12 1/2-inch-long leg in each bottom pedestal. Drive three screws through the pedestal into the leg. The bottom edge of the spreader rests on each pedestal between the notches. Make the end of the spreader flush with the outer face of each leg.

4 **FASTEN THE RAILS** to the undersides of the 2×6 seat boards with 2 1/2-inch-long deck screws. Rails are 16 inches long with 45-degree beveled ends. Position the outer faces of the 2×2 rails 4 1/2 inches from the board ends. Center the 2×4 rail on the seat boards. Each rail end is 1/2 inch from the board edge. Make a 1/4-inch-wide gap between seat boards.

5 **DRIVE SCREWS** through the 2×2 rails into the top pedestals. Position the seat on the pedestals for a 1/2-inch overhang on each long side. Rail positions create 1-inch overhangs at the ends.

BUILDING A BUILT-IN BENCH

BUILT-IN BENCH PERPENDICULAR TO JOISTS: Bolt or screw a 2×10 leg on one side of a joist at each end of the bench location. Space legs no more than four 16-inch-on-center joists apart. Cut and install rails and seat as shown in a parallel joist installation. Add blocking between joists to prevent the bench from rocking.

ADD A BORDER OF COLOR

Make railing planters to add floral color to your deck. Build them from 1× lumber of the same type of wood used on the deck. Space the sides to fit over the cap rail. Make butt joints between side, end, and bottom pieces. Fasten pieces together with deck screws. Drill several ½-inch-diameter drain holes in the bottom and attach small feet to the underside to provide air circulation.

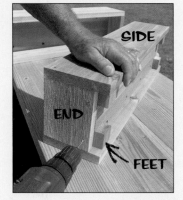

BUILT-IN BENCH PARALLEL TO JOISTS: Bolt or screw a 2×10 leg on both sides of the joist at each end of the bench location. Space the inside edges of the legs 30 inches apart for a 5-foot-long bench. Center and fasten a 16-inch-long 2×6 or 2×8 rail across the edges of each pair of legs (above, left). Make the top edge of a rail flush with the ends of the

legs. Miter the lower corners of the rails before installing. Attach 2×6 seat boards to the rails. Drive screws through additional rails installed on the underside of the boards (above, right) as shown on page 175. Attach cleats to the legs to support decking around the bench.

DECK ACCESSORIES

BUILDING A PRIVACY SCREEN

Attach posts for a privacy screen with the same methods used for railings—just cut longer posts. Posts also may be through posts or fastened to decking (see page 158). Posts installed on the deck may require permanent bracing. An average height for a privacy screen is 6 feet. Depending on the purpose for the screen, there are a variety of materials you can use. Use lattice for the screen as in this project if some sun and air movement are desired. Train a vining plant on the lattice for greater privacy. Install solid material such as tinted plastic or glass as a windbreak. Use fencing for greater privacy.

SKILL SCALE

EASY | MEDIUM | HARD

SKILLS: Measuring and cutting lumber and lattice, driving fasteners.

HOW LONG WILL IT TAKE?

PROJECT: Building three privacy screens, with two people to attach the posts.

EXPERIENCED . . . . . 4 HR.

HANDY . . . . 4.5 HR.

NOVICE . . . . 5 HR.

✓ STUFF YOU'LL NEED

TOOLS: Tape measure, straightedge, maul, hammer, nail set, circular saw, drill.

MATERIALS: Lumber, lattice, fasteners.

1 **INSTALL 2×4 FRAMING** across the tops of the posts. Space 4×4 posts 4 feet 3¾ inches apart on center for 4-foot-wide pieces of lattice. Attach bottom framing pieces between post faces. Position the lower face of bottom framing about 3 inches above decking to make it easy to clean the deck.

2 **ATTACH 1-INCH-WIDE STRIPS** of ⁵⁄₄ lumber to posts and framing. Snap a chalk line down the center of each inner face of posts and framing. Install strips along one side of the line only. Miter each strip end at 45 degrees before installing.

3 **INSTALL REMAINING STRIPS** after positioning lattice pieces. Use the strips to hold the lattice in place rather than driving fasteners through the lattice.

BUILDING AN ARBOR

Build an arbor with the same basic building methods used in deck building. Spacing of structural framing usually can be greater because of the lighter load—check with local code. The number of cover pieces depends on how much shade you desire. Install beams at different heights to make a sloping arbor roof. Make temporary braces from plywood weighted with concrete blocks. In some areas arbors are considered building structures. Check with local building officials to make sure the arbor you have planned meets code.

1 **INSTALL 4×4 POSTS** in post anchors. Attach the post anchors to the decking with screws.

TEMPORARY BRACING

2 **ATTACH DOUBLED 2×8 JOISTS** to the post tops with adjustable post caps. Install beams on the long sides of the arbor. Temporarily brace posts in position. Cut miters across lower beam board corners before installing, if desired.

3 **FASTEN PERMANENT 2×6 BRACES** to strengthen the beam and post frame.

4 **INSTALL 2×6 RAFTERS** across the beams with rafter ties. Space rafters 16 inches apart on center. Position each outer rafter so an additional 2×6 brace can be attached to the inside face and the post. Miter the rafter ends to match the beam ends before installing.

5 **ATTACH 2×2 COVER PIECES** with deck screws. Cut miters in the ends of the cover pieces before installing.

6 **NAIL TRIM PIECES** made from 1× lumber to cover the post anchors. Miter the ends of the trim pieces at 45 degrees and fasten them with galvanized finish or spiral shank nails. Drill pilot holes to prevent splitting.

7 **SANDWICH THE BEAM** boards around the posts and fasten with carriage bolts. Stagger the bolts on both sides of the center of each post to prevent splitting.

ATTACHING AN ARBOR TO A HOUSE

One side of an arbor may be the wall of a house. Install a ledger board at the appropriate height (see pages 42–43). Attach one end of the rafters to the ledger board with joist hangers. Use a bevel gauge to determine the trimming angle for rafters that slope down from the ledger board (near left). Trim the end of a rafter and attach it with a skewable joist hanger (far right).

LOW-VOLTAGE LIGHTING INSTALLATION TIPS

Low-voltage lighting is available in ready-to-install kits and as individual lights. Surface-mounted lights are easier to install than recessed lights, but you can create a more finished look with recessed lights. Spend some time looking at the outdoor lighting options available and determine the effect you want to create with outdoor lights. Low-voltage lighting installations usually aren't covered by local code because low voltage isn't considered dangerous. The only regular voltage necessary is a GFCI receptacle to plug in the low-voltage unit. Safety Note: Have a professional install a GFCI if you're not confident of your electrical skills. Follow the manufacturer's installation directions for the product you purchase. Most units install easily with connections snapping together.

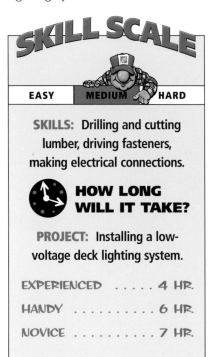

SKILL SCALE

EASY **MEDIUM** HARD

SKILLS: Drilling and cutting lumber, driving fasteners, making electrical connections.

HOW LONG WILL IT TAKE?

PROJECT: Installing a low-voltage deck lighting system.

EXPERIENCED . . . . . 4 HR.

HANDY . . . . 6 HR.

NOVICE . . . . 7 HR.

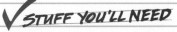

STUFF YOU'LL NEED

TOOLS: Tape measure, hammer, drill, jigsaw, screwdriver, stripper, lineman's pliers.

MATERIALS: Low-voltage lighting system, cable staples, GFCI receptacle, outdoor electrical box.

CONNECT THE LOW-VOLTAGE CIRCUIT WIRES to the transformer terminals. Attach the low-voltage lighting system transformer near a GFCI receptacle. Install the GFCI in an exterior-rated electrical box designed for permanent plug-in use.

FASTEN CIRCUIT WIRES to deck framing with exterior-rated wire staples. Route wires on the underside of the deck, underneath railings, or on the back sides of posts as much as possible.

RUN WIRES THROUGH HOLES drilled inside stairs or other covered locations. Or conceal holes in the seams where decking butts against posts or other framing.

INSERT RECESSED LIGHT UNITS into holes cut in stair risers, perimeter joists, or railing. Position lights to best illuminate stairs and other passageways.

DECK FINISHING, MAINTENANCE, & REPAIRS

No deck is maintenance-free. Applying a finish on a wood deck ensures that it will last longer and look its best. Climates with the greatest range of weather conditions increase the amount and frequency of maintenance. Following are methods that show you how to clean and renew your deck to keep it looking its best. See pages 184–185 to identify problems on an existing deck. You may be able to make a few easy repairs. Otherwise, learn how to safely tear down an old deck before building a better one in its place.

CHAPTER TEN PROJECTS

APPLYING FINISH

Apply outdoor deck stain to cover the green color of pressure-treated wood (page 13). Also use stain when you want to match the color of the deck to the house siding or trim. Opaque stains provide the best color coverage of the wood. However, they may peel and require frequent reapplication. Semitransparent stains soak deeply into wood fibers and wear well for longer periods, and they allow more of the wood tone and grain to show. Clear sealers or wood preservatives are good choices for cedar and redwood. They provide protection without diminishing the natural beauty of the wood. Choose a finish product containing mildew prevention. A clear sealer or preservative must have UV inhibitors or sunlight will break it down and affect wood color. Paint usually isn't the best finish choice because traffic areas quickly show wear. It also requires more frequent maintenance.

Apply one thin coat of finish to penetrate and dry completely. Thick layers of finish don't penetrate nor dry completely. The wood should be dry before applying finish. Sprinkle a little water on the deck. If it soaks in immediately, the wood is dry enough for finish application. New pressure-treated lumber must dry out completely before finish is applied. Check with the lumber supplier for the proper amount of drying time.

Make sure whatever finish you apply is rated for outdoor use and for a deck surface. Follow manufacturer's application instructions for best results. And don't spray or paint yourself into a corner.

Use a deck brightener to clean a deck before applying new finish (page 184). A brightener removes dirt, mildew, and the top layer of sun-faded wood fibers to restore the natural color of cedar and redwood.

Reapply finish to decks approximately once a year. Harsh climates and heavy deck usage may require reapplication twice a year.

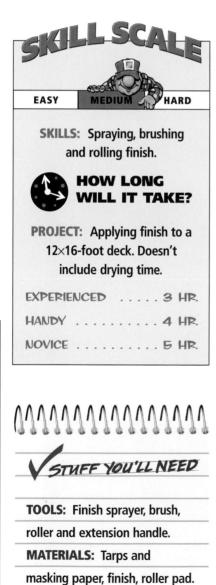

SKILL SCALE

EASY | MEDIUM | HARD

SKILLS: Spraying, brushing and rolling finish.

HOW LONG WILL IT TAKE?

PROJECT: Applying finish to a 12×16-foot deck. Doesn't include drying time.

EXPERIENCED . . . . . 3 HR.

HANDY . . . . 4 HR.

NOVICE . . . . 5 HR.

✔ STUFF YOU'LL NEED

TOOLS: Finish sprayer, brush, roller and extension handle.

MATERIALS: Tarps and masking paper, finish, roller pad.

BUYER'S GUIDE

SPRAY-ON SEALER

Use a hand-pumped sprayer or an electric power sprayer to evenly apply clear sealer, stain, or paint. Use an electric sprayer for large deck areas. Follow manufacturer's directions for use and plan to back-roll and back-brush after spraying the finish material. Spray finish on a windless day and cover shrubs and other objects with tarps.

HAND-PUMPED SPRAYER

POWER SPRAYER

1 **APPLY FINISH MATERIAL** with a sprayer. Use a hand-pumped unit for small deck areas, apply finish on small decks with a roller and brush. Use a roller on decking after spraying to force finish into the wood and to spread out any pooled material. This method is called back-rolling.

2 **USE A BRUSH** to work the finish into end grain, seams, and gaps between boards. This method is called back-brushing. Back-brush vertical surfaces to remove drips. End grain soaks up finish, and you may need to apply more.

CLEANING A DECK

1 **REMOVE LOOSE PAINT** or opaque stain with a paint scraper. Scrape down damaged areas to bare wood. Then sand each area to feather the edges of remaining finish material down to bare wood.

2 **USE A STIFF-BRISTLE BRUSH** to remove flaking stain or dirt. Don't use a metal-bristle brush on cedar or redwood because the metal bristles may scar soft wood surfaces and rust if they get imbedded into the wood.

3 **APPLY A DECK BRIGHTENER** product to wood surfaces. Mix the product according to manufacturer's directions. Work the brightener into the wood with a stiff-bristle brush, using an extension handle on the brush, if necessary.

4 **WASH THE DECK SURFACES** to remove brightener solution and other residue, using a power washer with a fan spray nozzle. The extra pressure of this tool is necessary to adequately clean the deck. Let the deck dry thoroughly before applying new finish. Be careful power washing a cedar deck. Use the low power setting to avoid damaging the wood.

DECK EXAMINATION TIPS

REPAIR LOOSE OR DAMAGED DECKING. Loose fasteners, such as popped nailheads, can be hammered back in. Replace boards that are severely cupped or deteriorating.

POKE THE TIP of a narrow-blade screwdriver into suspect areas. Wood that the tip easily penetrates is rotting.

CHECK FOR OVERCUT NOTCHES on open stair stringers (see page 138–140). Replace dangerously weak stringers with overcut notches (note the saw kerfs extending past the notch).

DECK FINISHING, MAINTENANCE, & REPAIRS

DECK EXAMINATION TIPS (CONTINUED)

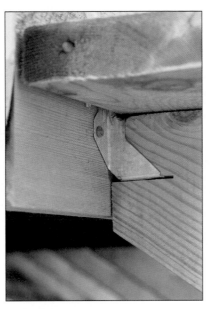

EXAMINE STAIR STRINGERS for misaligned notches and treads or tread runs under 10 inches. The stringer shown does not support treads properly.

IMPROPERLY FASTENED STRINGERS must be replaced. A slot cut for a standard joist hanger in the top end of the stringer, as shown, has seriously weakened the stringer. Toenailing also is not an adequate fastening method.

DECKING THAT FALLS SHORT of framing along a deck perimeter may form a moisture trap. Wood may deteriorate quickly in these spots.

EXAMINE THE LEDGER for signs of water damage or rot. Presence of either of these usually indicates absent or improperly installed flashing.

MEASURE THE SPACING between balusters and beneath bottom rails. Gaps greater than 4 inches are a code violation and are potentially dangerous.

LOOK FOR MILDEW OR MOLD on wood surfaces. These generally can be removed with a thorough cleaning (see page 184).

REPAIRING A DECK

epair and maintenance needs for a well-built deck less than 10-15 years old are few. They usually involve resetting some fasteners, replacing a few pieces of decking, cleaning the deck to remove dirt and mildew, or reapplying finish. An older deck, especially one included in a home purchase, may have more problems. Moisture damage or rot in deck framing indicate that it is time for a new deck. One deteriorating joist or post usually indicates that more will soon follow. Replace a deck if an examination reveals several of the problems shown on pages 184–185.

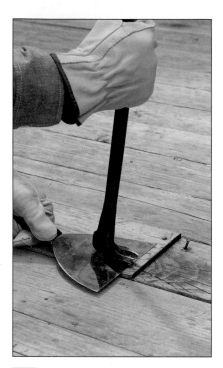

1 **REMOVE LOOSE OR POPPED NAILS** with a cat's paw (above, left) or pry bar. Protect the board surface with a wide putty knife. Drive long deck screws in place of the nails (above, right). Drill pilot holes and use additional screws if necessary.

2 **DRIVE THE CLAWS** of a cat's paw underneath nailheads to pry them out when removing damaged decking (above, left). Use a pry

bar to lift out damaged boards (above, center). Protect adjacent boards with a wide putty knife. Cut and install replacement boards. Let

a new board overhang at the edge of a deck (above, right); it's quicker and more accurate to trim in place than to trim before installing.

TEARING DOWN AN OLD DECK

Replacing a worn-out or poorly built deck requires that it first must be removed. Make this as simple and quick as possible by cutting apart the deck. Have a refuse hauler drop a large waste container as close to the site as possible. Cut the deck into pieces you can easily carry and place into the container. Tell the hauler what material will be placed in the container. Many municipalities charge extra for pressure-treated lumber. Don't mix yard or household waste with construction refuse.

Work safely while demolishing a deck. Have a helper support long joists, beams, and posts, if necessary. Wear safety glasses and a dust mask. Make certain you have stable footing when operating saws. Tear down a deck in the sequence shown below and on page 188. Tear down lower deck levels on multilevel decks first. Wear work gloves to protect your hands from splinters and sharp edges. Wear work boots rather than sneakers or other lightweight shoes. Demolition of a high deck or one on a steep slope is better left to a professional.

Check with local code before you begin demolition. Some codes require leaving part of the original structure if you want to replace an existing deck.

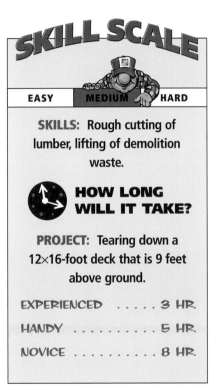

SKILL SCALE

EASY — MEDIUM — HARD

SKILLS: Rough cutting of lumber, lifting of demolition waste.

HOW LONG WILL IT TAKE?

PROJECT: Tearing down a 12×16-foot deck that is 9 feet above ground.

EXPERIENCED	. . . . .	3 HR.
HANDY	. . . .	5 HR.
NOVICE	. . . .	8 HR.

✓ **STUFF YOU'LL NEED**

TOOLS: Reciprocating saw, circular saw, pry bar.

MATERIALS: Waste container.

1 **CUT RAILINGS** into 4- to 6-foot-long sections with a reciprocating saw. Install a blade for fast, rough cuts in the saw. Trim balusters attached to perimeter joists at decking level.

2 **USE A CIRCULAR SAW** to cut through decking along both sides of each joist. Snap chalk lines to guide the cuts. Remove stair treads and riser boards with a hammer and pry bar.

3 **CUT EACH STRINGER** at the top end with a reciprocating saw. You should be able to pry it off a toe kick or other fasteners at the bottom end.

4 **USE A RECIPROCATING SAW** to cut each joist just inside the joist hangers or other fasteners. Begin each cut at the top edge of a joist.

5 **CUT THROUGH POSTS** just underneath the beams, using a reciprocating saw. Install a blade long enough to pass completely through the post.

6 **USE A PRY BAR** to pry the ledger from the house after screws and bolts are unfastened. Also remove old flashing if present. Check for damaged sheathing or framing behind the ledger before installing a new ledger.

INDEX